GREAT AMERICAN COOKIES

GREAT AMERICAN COOKIES

Lorraine Bodger

A Jane Ross Associates Book

ARCO PUBLISHING, INC.
New York

Published by Arco Publishing, Inc.
215 Park Avenue South, New York, NY 10003

Book design and illustrations by Lorraine Bodger

Library of Congress Cataloging in Publication Data
Bodger, Lorraine.
    Great American cookies.
    "A Jane Ross Associates book."
    Includes index.
    1. Cookies. I. Title.
TX772.B63 1985   641.8'654   85-6209
ISBN 0-668-06507-9

Printed in the United States of America

I would like to acknowledge, with thanks,
the contributions of the following people:
Annie Wright and Liz Sanchez, professional chefs
and recipe testers; Delia Ephron; Claire Javna;
Maggie Javna; Jane Ross; Nina Salamon;
Kathleen Sizemore; Blanche Small.

Contents

1. MAKING COOKIES

I don't know about you, but when I head for the kitchen with cookies on my mind, I'm thinking complicated thoughts. Since I'm the one who will bake them, I've got to consider a lot of issues.

How much time do I have to devote to this project? How much energy? Who else will be eating the cookies? Perhaps I have a definite purpose in mind, like an upcoming party or bake sale—what would be fun and appropriate to make? Or do I feel a chocolate attack coming on? Maybe I'm just craving comfort in the shape of a little round baked goody. All these bits of information are the stuff of which recipe choices are made. Cookies, I find, are a surprisingly emotional subject.

So with all these vital questions to answer, why are most cookie cookbooks organized into chapters titled Rolled Cookies, Molded Cookies, Pressed Cookies and Refrigerator Cookies? It's certainly interesting to know the basic types of cookies, but those are not the categories relevant to my choice of recipe. I'd rather know where to find a quick-to-make cookie, a chocolate cookie, a favorite or traditional cookie, cookies for Christmas or snacks or rainy afternoons at home with the kids. I'll bet you would, too, so here it is. *Great American Cookies*, the cookie cookbook that faces up to the real needs of daily life. I hope it serves you as well as it is serving me.

Utensils and equipment

What do you really need for cookie baking? Chances are you already own most of the basic equipment.

For measuring

Graduated measuring cups for dry ingredients
Glass measuring cup with clear markings and a well-made lip, for
    liquid ingredients
Graduated measuring spoons

For mixing

Small and large mixing bowls
Wooden spoons for hand mixing
Electric mixer (hand-held is fine) with low, medium and high speeds
Rubber spatula for scraping down the sides of the bowls

For baking

Oven thermometer (mercury type) for checking and adjusting oven
    temperature
Timer
Cookie sheet: This is the most important utensil for successful cookie
    baking. Invest in two shiny (not dark), heavy-weight sheets in
    a size that fits on your oven rack with at least 2 inches clear-
    ance on all sides. The best cookie sheet has a rim at one or
    both ends, unlike a jelly roll pan, which has a rim running
    around all four sides. Most cookbooks advise against using
    jelly roll pans as cookie sheets, claiming that the rims make it
    difficult to remove the cookies and also cause uneven baking.
    I have, however, used my jelly roll pans for years with no
    adverse effects on my cookies. Remember, you can turn a jelly
    roll pan or any other heavy baking pan wrong side up and
    use it in that position as a cookie sheet.

Baking pans in standard sizes for bar cookies (see recipes for exact measurements)
Metal spatula for removing cookies from the cookie sheet
Wire racks, raised on wire feet, for cooling the cookies

For special operations

Rolling pin
Cookie cutters
Cookie press with an assortment of disks
Pastry bag with a few large and small tips
Fluted pastry wheel for cutting decorative edges

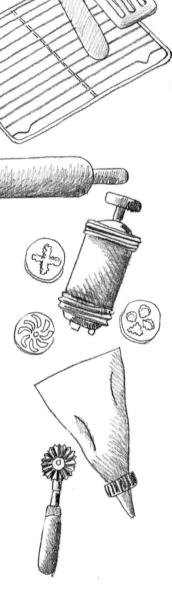

Ingredients

It is important for you to know what ingredients I have used in testing the recipes in this book so that you can duplicate them accurately or make informed choices about altering the ingredients.

Butter

I use unsalted (sweet) butter for making cookies. However, if you happen to have only lightly salted butter around, you may certainly use it. It won't make an appreciable difference in the taste, especially if you reduce by about half any salt called for in the recipe.

You must use sticks of butter, not whipped butter.

Margarine

There seem to be two camps lined up on the margarine issue. One camp says it just can't be substituted for butter and the other says go ahead and use it. It can become a real consideration if you are concerned about your health and your wallet.

No one expects margarine to taste like butter, but you can still make good cookies with it—particularly when it's used in doughs with strong flavors like chocolate, pumpkin or cinnamon. A good compromise is to use half butter and half margarine. Unsalted margarine is excellent for greasing your cookie sheets and baking pans.

Always use sticks of margarine, never whipped margarine.

Sugar

When you see sugar in the list of ingredients of a recipe in this book, it means plain, ordinary, white, granulated sugar.

If brown sugar is listed, that means you may take your choice of light brown or dark brown sugar. When it is important to use one or the other, the list of ingredients will specify light or dark.

Confectioners' sugar is another name for powdered sugar or 10X sugar.

Other sweeteners—like honey, molasses or corn syrup—show up in some recipes. Don't make the mistake of thinking you can substitute one of them for sugar, because it just won't work.

Flour

Use regular, all-purpose flour and don't sift it unless the recipe specifically calls for you to do so. Instead of sifting, spoon it lightly into the measuring cup and level off with a knife. Never, never tap the measuring cup to even off the top; you'll wind up with too much flour.

Don't use cake flour (a soft-wheat flour) unless it's called for, because it's not the same as all-purpose flour (milled from a combination of hard and soft wheats).

Eggs

Use large eggs in all recipes unless otherwise indicated. It's best to have them at room temperature.

Baking powder

First, the baking powder should be double-acting. Second, don't confuse it with baking soda, which is also often listed as an ingredient. Here's a tip: If you run out of baking powder, you can substitute 1 teaspoon of cream of tartar plus 1 teaspoon of baking soda for each teaspoon of baking powder needed.

Nuts

All kinds of nuts are called for in this book—walnuts, pecans, hazelnuts, pistachios, almonds, peanuts, cashews. Whatever kind of nut you are using, it must be fresh or it will ruin the taste of your cookies. Nuts can be chopped by hand with a knife or nut chopper, in a blender or food processor. The drawing will show you what I mean when I specify ground, finely chopped, chopped or coarsely chopped nuts.

Chopped or ground almonds can be made with your choice of almonds with the skins left on or with blanched (skinned) almonds. Here's how to blanch almonds: Put the almonds in a small pot and cover with boiling water. Let the almonds sit in the water for a few minutes. Drain the hot water out, rinse in cold water and drain again. One by one, pinch the loosened skins right off the almonds. (Be careful the nuts don't go shooting across the room when you pinch them.) Dry them first with paper towels and then in the oven at the lowest possible heat, until the almonds are crisp but not browned or burned.

Sometimes a recipe will call for "1 cup finely chopped walnuts"; this means you must chop some walnut halves and then measure out a cup of them. Other times a recipe will call for "1 cup walnuts, chopped"; this means you must measure a cup of walnut halves and *then* chop them.

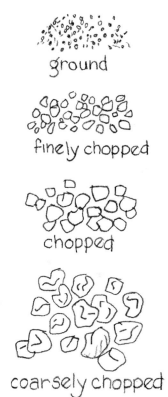

ground

finely chopped

chopped

coarsely chopped

1 cup finely chopped walnuts

1 cup walnuts, chopped

Chocolate and cocoa

Recipes may require unsweetened chocolate in squares or semi-sweet chocolate in squares or chips (also called morsels or bits). Use good-quality chocolate specifically intended for baking. Cocoa indicates unsweetened cocoa powder, not a mix of any sort.

Chocolate squares or chips may be melted, when required, either in the top of a double boiler or in a heavy saucepan over very low heat. The truth is that you can melt chocolate in a not-so-heavy saucepan over very low heat, too, if you watch it like a hawk and stir it constantly so it doesn't burn.

Other ingredients

Oatmeal: Always use the regular kind, never the quick-cooking or instant kind.

Raisins: Use dark ones unless otherwise specified; they should be soft, plump and seedless. If they are dry and hard, soak in very hot water for 15–20 minutes.

Other dried fruit: These should be soft and plump, too, but if they're not, soak them as described above.

Vanilla: Use real vanilla extract—no imitations.

Sweetened flaked or shredded coconut: This comes in a can or sealed plastic bag.

Grated orange or lemon rind: Grate only the very outer skin of the orange or lemon—the part that is brightly colored; be sure not to grate the bitter white pith right underneath.

Sherry and other alcoholic beverages: The alcohol content cooks away during baking, so you need not worry about giving the cookies to children or others who avoid alcohol.

Measuring the ingredients

Butter and margarine are easily measured by the tablespoon markings on the wrapper of each stick or by packing them firmly (no air bubbles) into a measuring spoon or cup. Sugar and other dry ingredients should be measured in graduated cups that can be leveled off at the top with a knife or spatula. Liquid ingredients should be measured in a clear glass or plastic cup with distinct markings: With the cup on a flat surface, fill it to the required amount. Then bend over (don't pick up the cup) and check it at eye level.

It is important to measure by these methods, but we all cheat now and then—for instance, measuring flour in a glass cup— and no tragedy will occur if you are very careful.

You also need a good set of measuring spoons that includes a tablespoon, teaspoon, ½ teaspoon and ¼ teaspoon.

Here are a few handy measurements:

Pinch = a little less than ⅛ teaspoon
3 teaspoons = 1 tablespoon
4 tablespoons = ¼ cup
8 tablespoons = ½ cup
16 tablespoons = 1 cup
¼ cup butter = 4 tablespoons = ½ stick
⅓ cup butter = 5⅓ tablespoons
½ cup butter = 8 tablespoons = 1 stick
⅔ cup butter = 10⅔ tablespoons
¾ cup butter = 12 tablespoons = 1½ sticks
1 cup butter = 16 tablespoons = 2 sticks

Making the dough

Ingredients—especially butter, unless otherwise noted— should be at room temperature. Quite often the butter and sugar must be creamed, and this is much easier to do if the butter is at room temperature (but not soft and melting). It is also much easier to do with an electric mixer, and that's how we tested all the recipes. You may perform all operations by hand if you like, but I recommend avoiding wear and tear by using a mixer. Medium speed is correct for creaming, mixing and blending. Whipping egg whites is done at high speed.

When flour is added to a creamed mixture, mix just enough to be sure the ingredients are well blended and no more; over-mixing toughens the dough.

Like you, I have been tempted at times to skip certain steps— like chilling the dough—in the interests of speed and gluttony. It has always been a mistake, so I strongly suggest that you follow the step-by-step directions for each recipe carefully to ensure good results.

Preparing the cookie sheet or baking pan

Cookie sheets and baking pans are either ungreased, greased or greased and floured. In the first case, do nothing to your clean cookie sheet or baking pan. In the second case, spread a very thin coat of unsalted butter or margarine (never use oil) on the sheet or pan with a pastry brush, a folded paper towel or a crushed piece of waxed paper. Be sure to get in the corners and don't miss any spots. In the third case, grease the sheet or pan as described above and then sprinkle a couple of tablespoons of flour into it. Holding the sheet or pan over the sink, tilt it back and forth while tapping it briskly to make the flour skitter all over the greased surface. Tap the excess flour into the sink.

Baking the cookies

There is a simple procedure for baking cookies, as you may know. Start like this: Shift one oven rack to the center of the oven. Put your oven thermometer on the rack and turn on the oven to the temperature indicated in the recipe. Let the oven heat for 15 minutes (set your timer to let you know when the oven is ready) and then check and adjust the temperature.

To bake cookies efficiently, you really must have two cookie sheets. Not, as some bakers would have it, to put two in the oven at once (counterproductive unless they fit side by side) but to work a sort of assembly line. Prepare both cookie sheets according to the requirements of the recipe and then follow this routine:

1. Fill one cookie sheet (Sheet A) with unbaked cookies (equally sized drops, slices, etc.). Pop it in the oven and SET THE TIMER.

2. While Sheet A is baking, fill the second cookie sheet (Sheet B). When the timer goes off, take Sheet A out and put Sheet B in. SET THE TIMER AGAIN.

3. Remove the baked cookies from Sheet A according to the recipe instructions, transferring them to wire racks to finish cooling.

4. Run cold water over the back of Sheet A and dry it with paper towels. (The cold water is essential; you must not put new

dough on a hot cookie sheet.) Turn Sheet A over and wipe away any crumbs. Grease again if necessary.

5. Fill Sheet A with unbaked cookies again. By this time the timer will ring. Remove Sheet B from the oven and start the process again.

Of course you may do all this in a leisurely fashion, but when you're in a hurry the system works wonders; if you move fast and keep moving, you can turn out dozens of excellent cookies in a very short time.

When are the cookies really done?

Sometimes it's hard to tell. First of all, during baking watch all the cookies carefully to be sure they don't burn or brown too much on the bottom. If your oven heats unevenly you may have to turn the cookie sheet back to front or adjust the placement of the oven rack.

Some cookies are soft when they come out of the oven and stay soft, others are soft when they are hot and become firm and crisp as they cool. Some come out crisp and remain so. The best advice I can give you is first, follow the recipe faithfully and second, take a cookie off the hot cookie sheet, wave it around to cool it and then taste it. If it's not done, return the cookie sheet to the oven for another minute or two and taste again.

Removing and cooling the cookies

Each recipe tells you when to remove the cookies from the cookie sheet after baking. Use a spatula for this step; I like a long, narrow, metal one but some bakers prefer a broad spatula. Loosen all the cookies on the cookie sheet at one time. If some of them harden and stick to the cookie sheet, put the sheet back in the oven for a minute and then you will be able to detach them more easily.

Transfer the cookies to wire racks, spreading them out in one layer. Do not pile them up or pack them away until they are perfectly cool or they will lose crispness and become soggy.

Bar cookies should be allowed to cool in the pan, which you must place on a wire rack. When the baked dough is completely cool, run a knife all around the edge to loosen the dough from the sides of the pan. Cut the dough into squares or bars as shown in the recipe and use a spatula to remove them very carefully from the pan.

Storing the cookies

If you care to look, you can find in various cookbooks exactly opposite points of view on the matter of which containers are appropriate for storing crisp cookies and which are for soft cookies. My cookies are generally not around long enough for it to make a great difference if the container has a loose- or tight-fitting lid. Besides, I always put about half the cookies in the freezer so I can surprise myself (and whoever happens to be around) with a lovely plate of cookies.

I like to keep all cookies in plastic containers with close-fitting lids; it doesn't seem to matter if the container is air-tight, because we keep opening the container anyway. It is important, however, to keep each kind of cookie in a separate container so the flavors don't get mixed. And never store crisp cookies and soft ones in the same container. (Cookies that become a little too soft can be crisped or freshened by heating them in the oven for a few minutes at about 300°.)

For freezing, I find that zip-lock plastic bags are handy for small numbers of cookies—perhaps the last 10 cookies of a batch you've been nibbling for days and can't stand the sight of any longer. I use plastic freezer containers for freezing larger amounts of cookies.

Bar cookies can be stored (or frozen) in plastic freezer containers or wrapped snugly in plastic in packets of four, eight or some other number convenient for your family.

Some frozen cookies are delicious while still frozen (for instance, Chocolate Chocolate Chip Cookies), but most are better when thawed: Spread them out in one layer and let them come to room temperature or warm them briefly in the oven at a low temperature and then let them cool off before you eat them.

How to use these recipes

Above all, you must—MUST—read the recipe from start to finish before you even take out a bag of flour. You may have to collect some special equipment (like cookie cutters or a pastry bag) or some special ingredients (like coconut extract or green crystal sugar) and there is nothing more maddening than discovering halfway through a baking session that you don't have whatever it is you need. So read the recipe first.

Next, *follow* the recipe, with good will and common sense. There are three important indications for each recipe, listed just above the ingredients. The first one tells you the approximate number of cookies or bars you can expect from the recipe. When I make Chocolate Crackles I use a ruler to be sure that the balls of dough I am shaping really are 1" in diameter—that's how I know I will get 5½ dozen cookies; if you just estimate the size of each ball, you may get 5½ dozen and you may get 4½ dozen. When the yield is 4½ dozen, each cookie will be a bit bigger than the recipe anticipates, so the baking time will be a little different, too. This is not a problem if you are an experienced baker because you will automatically alter the baking time; if you are inexperienced, stick to the recipe directions.

The second important indication tells you what baking pan to use and how to prepare it. (Be sure to read *Preparing the cookie sheet or baking pan* on page 16 for complete instructions.) It is essential to prepare the pan before you actually need it. On first consideration, that may seem silly. But on second thought, you will see that it makes for a smoother, more efficient operation if you have the pan ready and waiting to receive the cookies. However, do not prepare the pan too far in advance; if the dough must be refrigerated for several hours, it is not necessary to prepare the pan until shortly before you take the dough out of the refrigerator.

The same general advice holds true for the third important indication, the temperature to preheat the oven. Remember that the oven needs 15 minutes to preheat, so don't turn it on either too early or too late; try to have it at the right temperature when the cookies are on the cookie sheet, ready to be popped into the oven. A simple drop cookie dough takes only a short time to prepare, so turn on the oven before you begin mixing the ingredients. A rolled cookie dough will probably have to be chilled, so don't turn on the oven until about 15 minutes before taking the dough out of the refrigerator.

A word of encouragement

For the best results, do try to follow the recipe instructions carefully. However, don't be surprised by variations in such things as the softness of the dough, the number of cookies the recipe yields, the timing of the baking, the brownness of the finished cookies. There are many unpredictables in baking (like the condition of your flour and the accuracy of your oven) and you can expect them to affect your cookies on occasion.

Bake sales and bazaars

One of the best uses to which you can put cookies is to sell them at a bake sale or bazaar held for a worthy cause. With this important function in mind, I have listed some appropriate recipes below. The cookies in the list are great favorites (and therefore great sellers!); they're easy to make and look especially inviting at the baked goods booth at your local church hall or school gymnasium.

A short course on icing and piping

Simple piping is a snap to do, even if you've never tried it before. It's supposed to be fun—not a test of competency—so have a good time playing with the icing. This particular icing takes food coloring beautifully, is very easy to work with and dries hard and crisp. You will find a number of references to this section among the recipes in this book, and I'm sure you will find your own uses for the simple techniques, too.

When the cookies are baked, make one batch of icing and follow the piping instructions below.

Decorating Icing

Makes about 1⅔ cups

3½ cups (1 pound)
  confectioners' sugar
¾ teaspoon cream of tartar
3 egg whites
¼ teaspoon vanilla
¼ teaspoon almond extract

Stir the ingredients together in a deep bowl. Beat at high speed for 5 minutes. Keep the icing covered tightly with plastic wrap until you are ready to use it.

How to color the icing

Divide the icing into several small bowls, one bowl for each color (and plan to leave one white). Cover each bowl tightly with plastic wrap. Start with one bowl: Remove the wrap and add either a few drops of ordinary liquid food coloring or a tiny bit of paste coloring. Stir the coloring briskly into the icing. The more coloring you use, the darker or more intense the color will be—but proceed slowly, adding only a bit more color at a time. When you have the desired color, re-cover the bowl tightly with plastic. Repeat to make more colors.

Piping method #1:
Pastry bags with icing tips

This is one of two techniques for applying the icing to the cookies. (The second technique follows.) If you practice a little you will be able to produce a very professional, finished look using the pastry bag technique.

All you need is a pastry bag (used for icing as well as pastry) and two icing tips, #2 round tip and #27 star tip. The bag itself can be made of plastic or plastic-lined muslin; 10 inches is a good basic size. If you plan to do a lot of piping, it's efficient to have several bags so you can fill each one with a different color.

When you buy the pastry bags, be sure to buy a coupler for each bag. Follow the manufacturer's instructions—which should be included with your purchase—for putting together the pastry bag, coupler and #2 icing tip.

To fill the pastry bag with icing, fold the bag down over your hand to form a cuff as shown in the drawing. Hold the bag open and, using a small spatula or knife, fill the bag half-full of icing. Fold the cuff back up, fold the sides in and roll the end down. Grasp the folded end of the bag with one hand; with your other hand you will press out the icing and guide the flow from the tip.

Now you are ready to practice on some extra or imperfect cookies (or on a piece of waxed paper) with your filled pastry bag and round tip. Begin with a few straight lines: Hold the bag at about a 30-degree angle to the cookie or paper. Squeeze out the icing smoothly and steadily with one hand while moving your other hand to make the line. Try it a few more times. The tip should just barely touch the surface of the cookie; don't dig in or drag the tip.

Next try some little dots: Hold the bag perpendicular to the cookie with the tip just barely touching the surface. Squeeze out a little icing. When the icing forms a tiny mound, stop squeezing, lift up and move the tip away in a smooth motion. Make a whole row of dots to get comfortable with the technique.

Repeat these exercises with the star tip.

Now you can try some more acrobatic moves like scallops, loops, curlicues, bows and flowers.

Piping method #2:
Super-fast, no-mess plastic bags

This technique is ideal for children and it's pretty good for adults in a hurry, too. You can't get results that are as slick as you get with method #1, but method #2 is easier and neater. You can pipe lines, loops, dots, scallops and all kinds of curlicues—but you can't make the kinds of stars and flowers you can make with a pastry bag and star-shaped icing tip.

Method #2 is quite simple: Spoon each color of icing into a sturdy plastic food storage bag and push the icing down to one corner of the bag. Snip off a tiny, tiny bit of that corner, as shown in the drawing. Twist the bag tightly closed right over the icing. With one hand, hold the bag firmly at the twist; with the other hand, press out the icing and guide the flow from the snipped corner. Practice as described in the instructions for method #1.

If you get tired of piping, just put all the icing bags into a single plastic bag, close with a twist tie and stash in the refrigerator overnight.

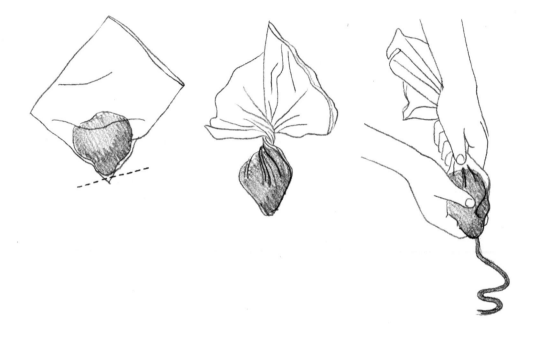

2. The Fastest, Easiest Cookies: DROP COOKIES

When time is of the essence—but you don't want to sacrifice quality—make drop cookies. In addition to tasting good, drop cookies are easy and quick to make. Just drop the dough onto a cookie sheet, pop in the oven, bake and eat. In this chapter you'll find a variety of flavors, some hearty, chunky cookies and even some elegant ones.

I always enjoy the sticky-finger method of making drop cookies, scooping up the dough with a teaspoon and pushing it off the spoon with my fingers. But if you prefer the clean-finger approach, you can drop the dough neatly and rapidly with two teaspoons, as shown in the drawing below.

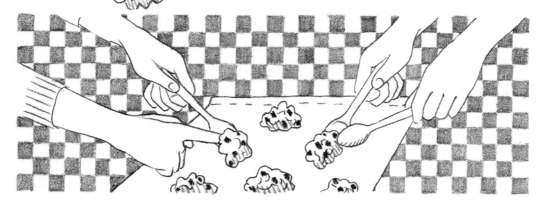

Vanilla Drops

This is a perfectly plain and tasty vanilla cookie, brown around the edges and slightly chewy in the center. Serve with fruit compote or a dish of berries and cream for a simple dessert.

Makes about 3 dozen cookies
Baking pan: greased cookie sheet
Preheat oven to 350°

¾ cup butter
1½ cups sugar
1 egg
1½ teaspoons vanilla
1¾ cups flour
¼ teaspoon salt

1. Cream the butter and sugar.

2. Add the egg and vanilla and blend well.

3. Stir together the flour and salt. Add to the creamed mixture and blend well.

4. Drop the dough by rounded teaspoons onto the cookie sheet, leaving 2 inches between drops.

5. Bake for 10 minutes. The cookies should be slightly browned around the edges. The centers may appear to be a bit undercooked, but they will firm up as they cool. Cool slightly on the cookie sheet and then transfer to wire racks to finish cooling.

Double Drop Cookies

If you like your vanilla perked up with a dab of chocolate, this is the cookie for you—a drop of vanilla dough melting into a drop of chocolate dough. It's crisp and chewy at the same time, and, because the vanilla dough spreads more than the chocolate, it's a little silly-looking. Kids love them.

Makes about 2½ dozen cookies

Baking pan: greased cookie sheet

Preheat oven to 350°

¾ cup butter or margarine
1½ cups sugar
1 egg, beaten
1½ teaspoons vanilla
1¾ cups flour
¼ teaspoon salt
1½ squares (1½ ounces) unsweetened chocolate, melted

1. Cream the butter and sugar.
2. Add the egg and vanilla and blend well.
3. Stir together the flour and salt. Add to the creamed mixture and blend well.
4. Divide the dough in half, in two separate bowls. Add the melted chocolate to one half and blend well.
5. To make each cookie, drop a teaspoon of vanilla dough onto the cookie sheet and a teaspoon of chocolate dough right next to it. Use a fork or spoon to push the two drops lightly together.

The easiest way to turn out a cookie sheet full of Double Drops is to put all the vanilla drops down and then put all the chocolate drops down next to them. Be sure you leave about 2 inches between cookies.

6. Bake for 10 minutes. Let the cookies cool for a minute and then transfer to wire racks to finish cooling.

Liz's Coconut Kisses

Liz Sanchez, a fine professional cook who worked on the testing of these recipes, contributed this one for the most mouth-watering coconut macaroon-type cookies I've ever had. They should be lightly browned on top and caramel-colored on the bottom to give that special toasted flavor.

Makes about 3 dozen cookies
Baking pan: greased cookie
    sheet
Preheat oven to 325°

1 cup sweetened condensed
    milk
2 teaspoons vanilla
1 teaspoon almond extract
¼ teaspoon cinnamon
3 cups sweetened flaked
    coconut

1. Stir together the condensed milk, vanilla, almond extract and cinnamon.
2. Add the coconut and mix well.
3. Drop the dough by teaspoons onto the cookie sheet, leaving 1 inch between drops.
4. Bake for 15 minutes. Remember to watch the cookies at the end of the baking period because the bottoms can burn very easily. Remove the cookies from the cookie sheet immediately and transfer to wire racks to cool.

Molasses Drops

This delicious cookie will flatten during baking to give a soft center with crisp edges.

Makes about 3 dozen cookies
Baking pan: greased cookie
    sheet
Preheat oven to 350°

½ cup butter
¾ cup brown sugar
1 egg
½ teaspoon vanilla
¼ cup molasses (not
    blackstrap)
1 teaspoon baking soda
1½ cups flour
pinch of salt

1. Cream the butter and brown sugar.
2. Add the egg and vanilla and blend well.
3. Stir together the molasses and baking soda. Add to the creamed mixture and blend well.
4. Stir together the flour and salt. Add gradually to the creamed mixture, blending well.
5. Drop the dough by teaspoons onto the cookie sheet, leaving 2 inches between drops.
6. Bake for 10 minutes. Allow the cookies to cool slightly on the cookie sheet and then transfer to wire racks to finish cooling.

Maggie's Cookies

My sister-in-law, Maggie Javna, invented this recipe one morning when a picnic was scheduled and she ran out of oatmeal for the oatmeal cookies. Twenty years from now my nephews, Gideon and Sam, will probably remember the cookies fondly as their childhood favorites. Family traditions have to start somewhere.

Makes about 2½ dozen
   cookies
Baking pan: greased and
   floured cookie sheet
Preheat oven to 350°

½ cup butter
½ cup sugar
½ cup brown sugar
1 egg
1 teaspoon vanilla
1 tablespoon milk
1 cup flour
1 teaspoon baking powder
½ teaspoon salt
½ cup raisins, optional
3 cups wheat flake cereal (the
   kind with no sugar added)

1. Cream the butter, sugar and brown sugar.
2. Add the egg, vanilla and milk and blend well.
3. Stir together the flour, baking powder and salt. Stir in the raisins, if desired. Add to the creamed mixture and blend well.
4. Stir in the wheat flake cereal.
5. Drop the dough by teaspoons onto the cookie sheet, leaving 2 inches between drops.
6. Bake for 10–12 minutes, until lightly browned. Let the cookies cool for about 3 minutes on the cookie sheet and then transfer to wire racks to finish cooling.

Kitchen Sink Cookies

The title and the list of ingredients tell the story: This cookie has everything—oatmeal, walnuts, dates, coconut and even chocolate chips, if you like. It's a fairly child-proof dough, too (not the least bit loose and sloppy), so let the kids take a turn making drops while you take a breather.

Makes about 4½ dozen
  cookies
Baking pan: greased cookie
  sheet
Preheat oven to 350°

1 cup margarine
½ cup sugar
½ cup brown sugar
2 eggs
¼ cup milk
2 cups flour
2 cups oatmeal (not the quick-
  cooking type)
1 teaspoon baking powder
½ teaspoon baking soda
1 teaspoon cinnamon
½ teaspoon salt
1 cup finely chopped walnuts
  or pecans
½ cup chopped dates
½ cup sweetened flaked
  coconut

1. Cream the margarine, sugar and brown sugar.

2. Add the eggs and milk and blend well.

3. Stir together the flour, oatmeal, baking powder, baking soda, cinnamon and salt. Add the nuts, dates and coconut and stir again. Add to the creamed mixture and blend well.

4. Drop the dough by rounded teaspoons onto the cookie sheet, leaving 1 inch between cookies.

5. Bake for 12–15 minutes. Let the cookies cool slightly on the cookie sheet and then transfer to wire racks to finish cooling.

Variation

Add ½ cup miniature chocolate chips at the same time you add the nuts to the flour mixture.

Sesame Rounds

What starts out as almost a batter—not quite a dough—becomes thin, crisp wafers with a very toasty sesame flavor. Sesame brittle, if there were such a thing, might taste like this. You must watch these cookies very closely while they are baking and allow them to become only the slightest bit browned around the edges.

Makes about 3½ dozen
   cookies
Baking pan: greased and
   floured cookie sheet
Preheat oven to 350°

2 eggs, beaten
2 tablespoons butter, melted
1½ teaspoons vanilla
¾ cup toasted sesame seeds
   (see toasting directions
   below)
1½ cups brown sugar
6 tablespoons flour
½ teaspoon salt

1. Stir together the beaten eggs, melted butter and vanilla.

2. Stir together the sesame seeds, brown sugar, flour and salt. Add to the egg mixture and blend well.

3. Drop the dough by teaspoons onto the cookie sheet, leaving 2 inches between drops.

4. Bake for 5 minutes, watching the cookies carefully to allow only slight browning around the edges. Remove the cookies from the cookie sheet almost immediately and transfer to wire racks to cool.

Toasted sesame seeds

In the oven: Spread the seeds on a shallow pan. Place in a 350° oven for about 20 minutes or until the seeds turn light brown.

On the stove: Place the seeds in a small skillet and cook over moderate heat, shaking and stirring, until they turn light brown.

With either method, watch the seeds carefully to be sure they don't burn.

Mountain Tops

I like to think that these cookies look like snowy peaks. They are, in fact, chocolate cookies crammed with nuts, topped with glaze and dunked in flaked coconut. The glaze is thick (to hold the coconut firmly), so use the tip of a spoon to push it into the crannies of the cookie.

Makes about 3½ dozen
　cookies
Baking pan: greased cookie
　sheet
Preheat oven to 350°

½ cup butter
1 cup sugar
3 squares (3 ounces)
　unsweetened chocolate,
　melted
2 eggs
2 teaspoons vanilla
1 cup flour
½ teaspoon salt
½ teaspoon baking powder
2 cups chopped nuts: walnuts,
　pecans, almonds, unsalted
　peanuts or any combination

Milk Glaze (page 165)
1–1½ cups flaked or shredded
　sweetened coconut

1. Cream the butter and sugar.
2. Add the melted chocolate and blend well.
3. Add the eggs and vanilla and blend well.
4. Stir together the flour, salt and baking powder. Add to the creamed mixture and blend well.
5. Stir in the nuts.
6. Drop the dough by rounded teaspoons onto the cookie sheet, leaving 1 inch between drops.
7. Bake for 12–15 minutes. Let the cookies cool on the cookie sheet for a minute or two and then transfer to wire racks to finish cooling.
8. Put the Milk Glaze in one bowl and the flaked coconut in another. When the cookies are cool, dip the top of each one first in Milk Glaze (using the tip of a spoon to push glaze into the crannies) and then in coconut.

Spiced Chocolate Drops

Here's a soft, cakelike drop cookie with a spicy taste that is light enough to let the chocolate flavor come through. The dough for these cookies is quite thin, so don't be surprised if it runs a bit when you drop it on the cookie sheet.

Makes about 4 dozen cookies
Baking pan: greased and
    floured cookie sheet
Preheat oven to 350°

½ cup butter
½ cup sugar
½ cup brown sugar
2 eggs
1 teaspoon vanilla
3 squares (3 ounces)
    unsweetened chocolate,
    melted
1½ cups flour
1 teaspoon baking powder
½ teaspoon baking soda
½ teaspoon salt
1 teaspoon cinnamon
¼ teaspoon ground cloves
¼ teaspoon nutmeg
½ cup buttermilk

1. Cream the butter, sugar and brown sugar.

2. Add the eggs, vanilla and melted chocolate and blend well.

3. Stir together the flour, baking powder, baking soda, salt and spices. Add the flour mixture and the buttermilk alternately to the creamed mixture. Blend well after each addition.

4. Drop the dough by teaspoons onto the cookie sheet, leaving 2 inches between drops.

5. Bake for 12 minutes. Allow the cookies to cool on the cookie sheet for a minute or two and then transfer to wire racks to finish cooling.

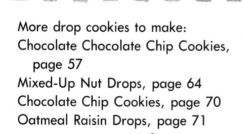

Cinnamon Drops

This is one of my favorites, great with or without nuts. These cookies have a distinct cinnamon taste, a good crunch (especially if you add the nuts) and pretty criss-cross tops made by the fork when you flatten them before baking. The tops should get firm during baking, but not brown. Don't let the edges brown, either.

Makes about 4 dozen cookies
Baking pan: ungreased cookie
   sheet
Preheat oven to 300°

1 cup butter
⅔ cup sugar
⅓ cup brown sugar
1 egg yolk
2 cups flour
1¼ teaspoons cinnamon
¼ teaspoon salt
1 cup chopped walnuts
   (optional)

1. Cream the butter, sugar and brown sugar.
2. Add the egg yolk and blend well.
3. Stir together the flour, cinnamon and salt. Add to the creamed mixture and blend well.
4. If you are using nuts, add them now and stir well.
5. Drop the dough by rounded teaspoons onto the cookie sheet, leaving 2 inches between drops. Flatten each cookie with a fork dipped in flour, pressing the dough once in each direction to make criss-cross lines.
6. Bake for 20–25 minutes. Let the cookies cool on the cookie sheet for a few minutes and then transfer to wire racks to finish cooling.

More drop cookies to make:

3. The Second-Fastest, Second-Easiest Cookies: BAR COOKIES

Banana Nut Bars
Nina's Plum Squares
Chocolate Chip Bars
Apple Cranberry Crumb Bars
Tipsy Raisin Bars
Magic Meringue Bars

Lemon Cream Cheese Squares
Pecan Pie Squares
Coconut Lime or Lemon Squares
Gold Bars
Butterscotch Bars

Bar cookies are made by spreading dough (and perhaps a filling) in a pan, baking and then cutting into cookie-size squares or rectangles, like brownies. They are indeed quick to make since there is no dropping, rolling out or molding of dough and the cookies are baked all at once rather than in batches on a cookie sheet. Bars are also a more substantial kind of cookie. One bar is about the same as two or three cookies, so they are great for brown bag lunches and snacks.

It is important to use a pan of the size specified in the recipe or the cookies will not come out as they should—the texture and baking time will be wrong and you risk failure and a waste of time and money. You may substitute a pan of equal or almost equal square inches—for instance, a 7 × 11 inch pan (77 square inches) for a 9 × 9 inch pan (81 square inches). But the surface area of standard baking pans varies greatly and you will be better off if you use the right one.

Banana Nut Bars

This is a moist, firm bar with real banana flavor, spiced with cinnamon and laced with chopped walnuts. Liz Sanchez, one of our recipe testers, tells me that these cookies are favorites of her teenaged son Daniel and his friends. One batch doesn't last long around her house.

Makes 35 bars
Baking pan: 15½" × 10½",
  greased and floured
Preheat oven to 350°

¾ cup butter or margarine
½ cup sugar
⅔ cup brown sugar
1 egg
1 teaspoon vanilla
2 cups mashed ripe bananas
  (about 4 medium)
2 cups flour
2 teaspoons baking powder
½ teaspoon salt
1 teaspoon cinnamon
¼ teaspoon nutmeg
1 cup chopped walnuts

1. Cream the butter, sugar and brown sugar.
2. Add the egg and vanilla and blend well.
3. Add the mashed bananas and blend well.
4. Stir together the flour, baking powder, salt and spices. Add to the creamed mixture and blend well.
5. Stir in the chopped nuts.
6. Spread the batter in the pan.
7. Bake for 25–30 minutes. The bars should be very slightly browned on the edges. Place the pan on a wire rack to cool and then cut in bars as shown in the drawing.

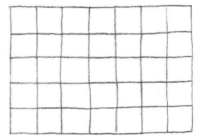

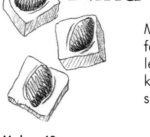

Nina's Plum Squares

My aunt Nina Salamon gave me this wonderful recipe for rich plum squares. The squares taste best when you let them rest in the refrigerator overnight—if you can keep them around that long. We make them with the small blue plums called Italian plums or prune plums.

Makes 40 squares
Baking pan: 13" × 9", greased and floured
Preheat oven to 350°

Bottom layer:
2 cups flour
⅔ cup sugar
¾ cup butter, softened
20 small blue plums (Italian plums or prune plums), cut in half the long way and pitted

Topping:
1 egg, beaten
¼ cup sugar
¾ cup sour cream
½ teaspoon vanilla

1. Make the bottom layer: Stir the flour and sugar together. Add the butter and mix with your hands until blended enough to form a ball of dough.

2. Pat the dough evenly into the pan, pressing it about ¼ inch up the sides.

3. Bake for 15 minutes, until the dough is brown at the edges and almost completely baked.

4. Place the plum halves on the baked dough, almost touching. The plums shrink during baking, so you will end up with half a plum in the middle of each square.

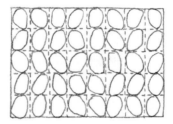

5. Make the topping: Mix together the egg, sugar, sour cream and vanilla until well blended.

6. Spread the topping carefully over the plums and baked dough.

7. Bake for 15–20 more minutes, until the plums are cooked. Cool overnight in the refrigerator and then cut into 40 squares, with a piece of plum in each.

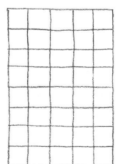

Chocolate Chip Bars

If you're too busy to make the drop cookies (there's a recipe for chocolate chip cookies on page 70), make the bars instead. They are chewy and yummy, a fine substitute for the real thing. Chocolate chip fans may even decide they prefer the bars.

Makes 24 bars
Baking pan: 9" × 9", greased and floured
Preheat oven to 350°

½ cup butter or margarine
¾ cup brown sugar
1 egg
1 tablespoon milk
1 teaspoon vanilla
1 cup flour
½ teaspoon baking powder
pinch of salt
1 cup (6 ounces) chocolate chips
¼–½ cup chopped walnuts or pecans

1. Cream the butter and brown sugar.
2. Add the egg, milk and vanilla and blend well.
3. Stir together the flour, baking powder and salt. Add to the creamed mixture and blend well.
4. Stir in the chocolate chips.
5. Spread the batter evenly in the pan and sprinkle with chopped nuts.
6. Bake for 25–30 minutes. Place the pan on a wire rack to let the dough cool and then cut into bars as shown in the drawing.

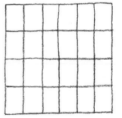

Apple Cranberry Crumb Bars

A bar for all seasons, especially autumn. A thin filling of apples and cranberry sauce makes this a tart, sweet treat and the crumb topping gives it a delightful crunch. There are two or three more steps to do than for some other bars, but the result is well worth the few extra minutes it takes.

Makes 21 bars
Baking pan: 11" × 7" × 2", greased
Preheat oven to 350°

Bottom layer:
6 tablespoons butter
¾ cup brown sugar
1 egg
2 cups flour
1 teaspoon baking powder
½ teaspoon salt

Filling:
1 tablespoon butter
2 tart apples, peeled and cored carefully, chopped fine
½ cup sugar
1 tablespoon flour
1 tablespoon lemon juice
1 tablespoon orange juice
½ cup canned whole cranberry sauce
dash of cinnamon

Crumb topping:
6 tablespoons butter
½ cup sugar
¾ cup flour
pinch of salt
¼ cup chopped walnuts

1. Make the dough for the bottom layer: Cream the butter and brown sugar. Add the egg and blend well. Stir together the flour, baking powder and salt. Add to the creamed mixture and blend well.

2. Pat the dough evenly into the pan, pressing it about ¼ inch up the sides.

3. Make the filling: Melt the butter in a saucepan. Add the chopped apples and cook at low heat until the apples soften (about 3 minutes). Add the remaining filling ingredients, stir well and bring to a boil. Reduce the heat and cook, stirring constantly, for 5 minutes. Set the filling aside to cool.

4. Make the crumb topping: With your hands or a food processor, blend the butter, sugar, flour and salt until crumbly. Add the chopped walnuts and blend briefly.

5. Spread the cooled filling over the dough in the pan. Sprinkle the crumb topping over the filling.

6. Bake for 30 minutes. Place the pan on a wire rack and let the dough cool. Cut in bars as shown and remove the bars carefully.

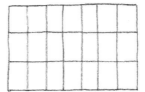

Tipsy Raisin Bars

Moist, raisin-studded cake, rich Vanilla Glaze, intense rum flavor—put them all together to make one of my favorite bar cookies. If you like the bars with a thick glaze (almost like frosting), let them cool before you spread the glaze on. If you prefer a thin coat of glaze, spread it on while the bars are still slightly warm. In either case, refrigerate the glazed pan of cookies for 10 minutes before cutting, to allow the glaze to firm up a bit.

Makes 35 bars
Baking pan: 13″ × 9″, greased and floured
Preheat oven to 350°

¾ cup raisins
½ cup light rum
¾ cup butter
½ cup sugar
1 egg
1 teaspoon vanilla
1½ cups flour
1 teaspoon baking powder
¼ teaspoon salt

Vanilla Glaze (page 165)

1. Soak the raisins in the rum for 1 hour. Pour off the rum (there should be about 6 tablespoons) and reserve.
2. Cream the butter and sugar.
3. Add the egg, vanilla and reserved rum and blend well.
4. Stir together the flour, baking soda and salt. Stir in the raisins. Add to the creamed mixture and blend well.
5. Spread the dough evenly in the pan.
6. Bake for 25 minutes. Place the pan on a wire rack to cool. Do not cut into bars yet.
7. For a thin coat, spread Vanilla Glaze on the dough while it is still warm. For a thick coat, allow the dough to cool completely and then spread the glaze. Place the pan in the refrigerator for 10 minutes to firm up the glaze. Remove from the refrigerator and cut into bars as shown in the drawing.

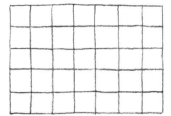

Magic Meringue Bars

The magic is in the meringue-and-nut topping. It takes you by surprise a short while after you remove it from the oven: The topping cools to become soft, rich and spicy in the middle, crisp and crunchy on top.

Makes 24 bars
Baking pan: 13″ × 9″, greased
Preheat oven to 350°

Bottom layer:
½ cup butter
¼ cup brown sugar
2 egg yolks
1 teaspoon vanilla
1¼ cups flour
1½ teaspoons baking powder
½ teaspoon salt

⅓ cup raspberry or apricot jam

Topping:
1 cup chopped walnuts or
**   pecans**
½ teaspoon cinnamon
2 egg whites
½ teaspoon vanilla
¾ cup brown sugar

1. Make the bottom layer: Cream the butter and brown sugar. Add the egg yolks and vanilla and blend well. Stir together the flour, baking powder and salt. Add to the creamed mixture and blend well.

2. Spread the dough evenly in the pan.

3. Carefully spread a thin layer of jam on the dough.

4. Make the topping: Stir together the chopped nuts and cinnamon and set aside. Stir together the egg whites and vanilla and beat until the egg whites hold a soft peak. Gradually beat in the brown sugar until the mixture holds stiff peaks and all the sugar is dissolved. Stir in the nut mixture.

5. Spread the topping over the jam and dough in the pan.

6. Bake for 25–30 minutes. The top should be light brown; it will become crisp as the bars cool. Place the pan on a wire rack to cool and then cut in bars as shown in the drawing.

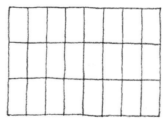

Lemon Cream Cheese Squares

You might suppose that these squares are like cheesecake, but they are not. They do have a crunchy, nutty crust plus a rich, dense topping with a nice, lemony flavor—but they don't have the customary heavy cream cheese taste. They make a great snack or light dessert.

Makes 16 squares
Baking pan: 9" × 9", greased and floured
Preheat oven to 350°

Bottom layer:
⅔ cup fine graham cracker crumbs
½ cup flour
¼ cup sugar
½ cup finely chopped walnuts
½ cup melted butter or margarine

Topping:
2 packages (3 ounces each) cream cheese, softened
⅔ cup sugar
2 eggs
1 tablespoon lemon juice
grated rind of one medium lemon
½ teaspoon vanilla
¼ cup flour
½ teaspoon baking powder

1. Make the bottom layer: Mix together the crumbs, flour, sugar and chopped nuts. Add the melted butter and blend well.

2. Pat the mixture evenly into the pan.

3. Bake for 12 minutes.

4. Make the topping: Blend the cream cheese and sugar until smooth. Add the eggs, lemon juice, grated rind and vanilla and blend well. Stir together the flour and baking powder. Add to the cream cheese mixture and blend well.

5. Pour the topping gently over the bottom layer.

6. Bake for 20 more minutes. Place the pan on a wire rack to cool and then cut in squares as shown in the drawing.

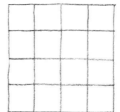

 Pecan Pie Squares

Luscious is the first word that comes to mind to describe these goodies. They have the classic pecan pie taste but they are even better, I think, because there is no thickener (like cornstarch) to interfere with the flavor and texture. They are very rich, so cut them in small squares.

Makes 36 squares
Baking pan: 9″ × 9″, greased
  and floured
Preheat oven to 350°

Bottom layer:
1 cup flour
½ cup brown sugar
½ cup butter

Topping:
2 eggs
½ cup light corn syrup
½ cup brown sugar
2 tablespoons melted butter
1 teaspoon vanilla
¼ teaspoon salt
¾ cup chopped pecans

1. Make the bottom layer: Stir together the flour and brown sugar. Cut the butter in with your hands until blended enough to form a ball of dough.

2. Pat the dough evenly into the pan.

3. Bake for 5–7 minutes. Place the pan on a wire rack to cool.

4. Make the topping: Beat the eggs. Add the corn syrup, brown sugar, melted butter, vanilla and salt and blend well. Stir in the chopped pecans.

5. Pour the topping over the dough in the pan.

6. Bake for 30 minutes. Place the pan on a wire rack to cool and then cut in squares as shown in the drawing.

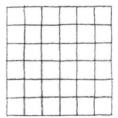

Coconut Lime or Lemon Squares

Conjure up the tropics with these lime or lemon bars. The bottom layer is like a cookie and the topping is tangy, with a creamy, chewy texture—thanks to the combination of eggs and sweetened, shredded coconut.

Makes 25 squares
Baking pan: 9" × 9", greased
Preheat oven to 350°

Bottom layer:
½ cup butter
¼ cup sugar
1¼ cups flour

Topping:
1 cup sugar
2 tablespoons flour
1 teaspoon baking powder
2 eggs, lightly beaten
2 tablespoons fresh lime juice
   for lime squares OR
2 tablespoons fresh lemon
   juice for lemon squares
2 teaspoons grated lime rind
   for lime squares OR
2 teaspoons grated lemon rind
   for lemon squares
⅓ cup sweetened shredded
   coconut
extra coconut for sprinkling on
   top

1. Make the dough for the bottom layer: Cream the butter and sugar. Add the flour and blend well.

2. Pat the dough evenly into the pan.

3. Bake for 15 minutes or until lightly browned. Cool in the pan on a wire rack.

4. Make the topping: Stir together the sugar, flour and baking powder. Add the eggs, lime (or lemon) juice, grated rind and coconut and blend well.

5. Spread the topping over the cooled dough. Sprinkle with a little more coconut.

6. Bake for 25–35 more minutes. The center should be firm and the edges will be lightly browned. Place the pan on a wire rack to cool and then cut in squares as shown in the drawing.

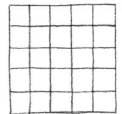

Gold Bars

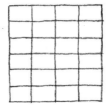

The golden colors of the ingredients give this recipe its name. It's an interesting combination—crisp cookie dough, spread with peach or apricot jam, topped with a soft, cakelike layer full of chopped apricots and almonds. The bars are tender, so remove them carefully from the pan.

Makes 24 bars
Baking pan: 8" × 8", greased
Preheat oven to 350°

Bottom layer:
½ cup butter or margarine
¼ cup sugar
1¼ cups flour

3 tablespoons peach or apricot jam, warmed

Topping:
2 eggs
¾ cup brown sugar
½ teaspoon vanilla
½ cup flour
½ teaspoon baking powder
pinch of salt
½ cup almonds, finely chopped
½ cup dried apricots soaked for 1 hour in water to cover, with a squeeze of lemon, and then finely chopped

1. Make the bottom layer: Cream the butter and sugar. Add the flour and blend well.
2. Pat the dough evenly into the pan.
3. Bake for 25 minutes, until lightly browned. Cool for a few minutes.
4. Spread the jam over the warm dough.
5. Make the topping: Beat the eggs, brown sugar and vanilla together. Stir together the flour, baking powder and salt. Add to the egg mixture and blend well. Stir in the chopped almonds and apricots.
6. Spread the topping over the jam and dough.
7. Bake for 25 more minutes. Place the pan on a wire rack to cool and then cut into bars as shown in the drawing.

Butterscotch Bars

Another super-simple, delicious bar cookie to make when you are in a big hurry. This is a thin bar, quite dense, with a lightly browned top. It's a real treat for butterscotch lovers.

Makes 36 bars
Baking pan: 13" × 9", greased and floured
Preheat oven to 350°

1 cup butter
½ cup sugar
½ cup brown sugar
2 egg yolks
1 tablespoon milk
1 teaspoon vanilla
2 cups sifted flour
1 teaspoon baking powder
1 teaspoon salt
1 cup (6 ounces) butterscotch chips

1. Cream the butter, sugar and brown sugar.
2. Add the egg yolks, milk and vanilla and blend well.
3. Stir together the flour, baking powder and salt. Add to the creamed mixture and blend well.
4. Stir in the butterscotch chips.
5. Spread the dough evenly in the pan.
6. Bake for 25–30 minutes. The top should be lightly browned. Place the pan on a wire rack and let the dough cool. Cut into bars as shown in the drawing.

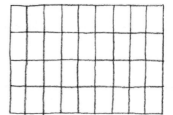

More bar cookies to make:
Delia's Brownies, page 55   Chewy Fruit Squares, page 126
Pecan Shortbread, page 63   Granola Bars, page 129

4. When Only Chocolate Will Do: CHOCOLATE COOKIES

Black and Whites
Chocolate Linzer Tarts
Chocolate Crackles
Chocolate and Marshmallow
    Sandwiches
Crisp Chocolate Pecan Cookies

Chocolate and Vanilla Twists
Sachertorte Cookies
Delia's Brownies
Mocha Fingers with Chocolate Sprinkles
Chocolate Chocolate Chip Cookies
Rum Truffles

It's absolutely true that when you want chocolate, no other flavor will do, and when chocolate occupies your mind, there's very little room for anything else. As a result, most passionate chocolate lovers are completely obsessed a good deal of the time. You want chocolate in every shape and form and you want it now.

Indulge yourself in the delectable variety of chocolate combinations in this chapter: chocolate with raspberry jam, chocolate with pecans, chocolate with chocolate and vanilla icing, rich chocolate brownies, chocolate with chocolate chips and more. There is chocolate in dense little balls, chocolate in crackly rounds, chocolate sandwiches, crisp chocolate twists, chocolate fingers with the ends dipped in—you guessed it—chocolate.

Serious chocoholics will have their own mysterious ways of deciding where to start, but you might do well to begin at the beginning of the chapter and work through to the end.

Black and Whites

When I was a child, I thought Black and Whites were the ultimate treat, a mysterious cookie that grew only in the bakery. If the bakery was closed, you were out of luck. How reassuring to grow up and discover home-made Black and Whites—so much better than any bakery cookie could possibly be, and easy to make, too.

Makes about 2 dozen cookies
Baking pan: greased cookie
  sheet
Preheat oven to 350°

½ cup butter
1½ cups sugar
1 egg
1 teaspoon vanilla
2½ squares (2½ ounces)
  unsweetened chocolate,
  melted
2½ cups flour
2 teaspoons baking powder
½ teaspoon salt
¼ cup milk

Chocolate Glaze (page 165)
Vanilla Glaze (page 165)

1. Cream the butter and sugar.
2. Add the egg and vanilla and blend well.
3. Add the melted chocolate and blend well.
4. Stir together the flour, baking powder and salt. Add to the creamed mixture alternately with the milk, blending well after each addition. Divide the dough in half, wrap each half snugly in plastic and refrigerate for 2–3 hours or until firm enough to roll out.
5. Dust the work surface and rolling pin with flour. Roll out half the dough at a time to a little more than ⅛ inch thick. Cut with a round cookie cutter 3½–4 inches in diameter. Lift away the excess dough and save for re-rolling. Transfer the rounds to the cookie sheet, leaving 1 inch between them.
6. Bake for 8–10 minutes. Let the cookies cool slightly on the cookie sheet and then transfer to wire racks to finish cooling.
7. Use a small spatula to spread Chocolate Glaze on one half of each cookie and Vanilla Glaze on the other half. Let the glazes harden.

Chocolate Linzer Tarts

A Linzer tart is a pair of cookies with raspberry jam between them, a cut-out in the top cookie and a sprinkling of confectioners' sugar. A chocolate Linzer tart is a pair of chocolate cookies put together the same way.

Makes about 2½ dozen
   sandwiches (5 dozen
   cookies)
Baking pan: greased cookie
   sheet
Preheat oven to 350°

1½ cups butter
¾ cup sugar
1 egg
1 teaspoon vanilla
3 cups flour
6 tablespoons unsweetened
   cocoa (not cocoa mix)
raspberry jam
confectioners' sugar

1. Cream the butter and sugar.
2. Add the egg and vanilla and blend well.
3. Stir together the flour and cocoa. Add to the creamed mixture and blend well. Divide the dough in half, wrap each half snugly in plastic and refrigerate for 2–3 hours or until firm enough to roll out.
4. Sprinkle flour generously on the work surface and rolling pin. Roll out half the dough at a time to ⅛-inch thick. Cut the dough with a scalloped cookie cutter 3 inches in diameter. Cut a 1-inch-diameter round from the center of half the 3-inch rounds. Gather up the excess dough and save it for re-rolling. Transfer the cookies to the cookie sheet, leaving 1 inch between them.
5. Bake for 10 minutes. Allow the cookies to cool slightly on the cookie sheet and then transfer to wire racks to finish cooling.
6. Spread the whole rounds with jam and cover with the cut-out rounds. Sprinkle with confectioners' sugar sifted through a fine strainer.

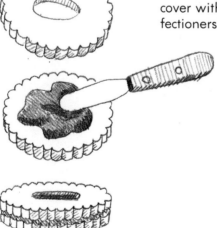

Chocolate Crackles

I made these recently with an eight-year-old space cadet named Adam Kass. I rolled the dough into balls and Adam dunked them in a bowl of confectioners' sugar and launched them from the bowl onto the cookie sheet, while keeping up a steady flow of conversation with mission control (me). The result of the project was about 5½ dozen perfect Chocolate Crackles, soft on the inside and crunchy on the outside, which Adam and his sister Julie proceeded to polish off at the speed of light.

Makes about 5½ dozen
  cookies
Baking pan: greased cookie
  sheet
Preheat oven to 350°

6 tablespoons butter
3 squares (3 ounces)
  unsweetened chocolate,
  melted
1½ cups sugar
2 eggs
1½ teaspoons vanilla
1½ cups flour
1½ teaspoons baking powder
¼ teaspoon salt
confectioners' sugar

1. Cream the butter until light and fluffy.
2. Add the melted chocolate and sugar and blend well.
3. Add the eggs and vanilla and blend well.
4. Stir together the flour, baking powder and salt. Add to the creamed mixture and blend well. Refrigerate for 3 hours or until firm.
5. Shape the dough into balls about 1 inch in diameter. Dredge each ball in a small bowl or plastic bag of confectioners' sugar to coat it thoroughly and place it on the cookie sheet, leaving 2 inches between balls.
6. Bake for 10–12 minutes, taking care not to burn the bottoms. The cookies may seem slightly underdone in the centers when you first take them out of the oven, but they firm up as they cool. Let the cookies cool on the cookie sheet for 5 minutes and then transfer to wire racks to finish cooling.

Chocolate and Marshmallow Sandwiches

Marshmallow topping seems to have a life of its own; it melts and oozes and won't stay where you put it. While we were trying to tame it, we invented this recipe for a marshmallow sandwich cookie (chocolate, of course) with the edge dipped in chocolate glaze that hardens and keeps the marshmallow from escaping.

Makes about 2 dozen
  sandwiches (4 dozen
  cookies)
Baking pan: greased cookie
  sheet
Preheat oven to 400°

½ cup butter
1 cup sugar
1 egg
1½ teaspoons vanilla
2 squares (2 ounces)
  unsweetened chocolate,
  melted
1¾ cups flour
1 teaspoon baking powder

Marshmallow topping (use any
  good commercial variety)

Chocolate Glaze (page 165)

1. Cream the butter and sugar.
2. Add the egg and vanilla and blend well.
3. Add the melted chocolate and blend well.
4. Stir together the flour and baking powder. Add to the creamed mixture and blend well.
5. Divide the dough in half and shape each half into a log about 1½ inches in diameter. Wrap each log snugly in plastic and refrigerate until firm. You may place the logs in the freezer to speed up the process.
6. Unwrap one log at a time and cut an even number of slices ⅛ inch thick. Place the slices on the cookie sheet, leaving 1 inch between them.
7. Bake for 12–15 minutes. Let the cookies cool for a minute or two on the cookie sheet and then transfer to wire racks to finish cooling.
8. To make one sandwich, turn one cookie wrong side up and put a generously rounded teaspoon of marshmallow topping on it. Cover with a second cookie, right side up, and compress the cookies to spread the filling evenly. Refrigerate for 10 minutes and then carefully roll the edge of the sandwich in *warm* Chocolate Glaze. The glaze will harden almost immediately, holding the marshmallow securely inside the sandwich. Thin the glaze periodically to maintain the consistency that is best for covering the edge of the sandwich.

Crisp Chocolate Pecan Cookies

Here's a plain, simple, delicious refrigerator cookie, suitable for continuous munching.

Makes about 5 dozen cookies
Baking pan: greased and
    floured cookie sheet
Preheat oven to 400°

½ cup butter
1 cup sugar
1 egg
2 tablespoons milk
1 teaspoon vanilla
2 squares (2 ounces)
    unsweetened chocolate,
    melted
2¼ cups flour
1½ teaspoons baking powder
¼ teaspoon salt
¾ cup finely chopped pecans

1. Cream the butter and sugar.
2. Add the egg, milk and vanilla and blend well.
3. Add the melted chocolate and blend well.
4. Stir together the flour, baking powder, salt and chopped pecans. Add to the creamed mixture and blend well.
5. Divide the dough in half and form each half into a log about 2 inches in diameter. Wrap each log snugly in plastic and refrigerate or freeze the dough until firm.
6. Unwrap the dough and cut slices ⅛ inch thick. Place the slices on the cookie sheet, leaving ½ inch between them.
7. Bake for 8–10 minutes, taking care not to let the cookies burn on the bottom. They are done even if they seem a little soft in the center. Let the cookies cool slightly on the cookie sheet and then transfer to wire racks to finish cooling.

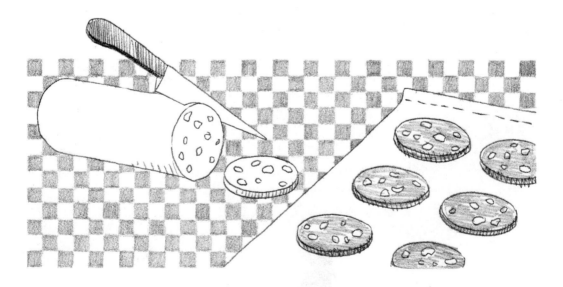

Chocolate and Vanilla Twists

For the folks who choose the ice cream cup with half chocolate and half vanilla, the black and white soda, the vanilla cake with chocolate icing or the chocolate cake with vanilla icing—a chocolate and vanilla cookie. The twists are very easy to make once you get into the swing of it.

Makes about 4 dozen cookies
Baking pan: ungreased cookie
   sheet
Preheat oven to 325°

¾ cup butter
¾ cup sugar
1 egg
2½ teaspoons vanilla
2 cups flour
½ teaspoon baking powder
¼ teaspoon salt
3 tablespoons unsweetened
   cocoa (not cocoa mix)

1. Cream the butter and sugar.
2. Add the egg and vanilla and blend well.
3. Stir together the flour, baking powder and salt. Add to the creamed mixture and blend well.
4. Divide the dough in half. Mix the cocoa into one half. Wrap or cover each half snugly with plastic and refrigerate for 3 hours or until very firm.
5. Break off a small piece of chocolate dough and a small piece of vanilla dough. Roll each piece into a rope about ½ inch in diameter. Cut the ropes to 3 inches long. Twist the two ropes together as shown in the drawing. Transfer the twist to the cookie sheet, using a spatula if necessary. Repeat with the remaining dough, working quickly.
6. Bake for 13 minutes. Let the twists cool slightly on the cookie sheet and then transfer to wire racks to finish cooling.

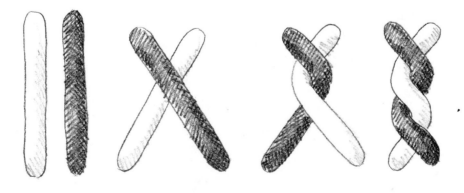

Sachertorte Cookies

Each fine-grained, delicate chocolate cookie is topped with traditional Sachertorte ingredients—apricot jam, semi-sweet chocolate and a bit of candied cherry. These handsome cookies can be assembled quickly because they are sliced from a roll of dough you can keep stashed in the refrigerator; the toppings just require a little heating up.

Makes about 2 dozen cookies
Baking pan: ungreased cookie
   sheet
Preheat oven to 350°

½ cup butter
½ cup sugar
1 egg yolk
1 teaspoon vanilla
3 tablespoons milk
2 squares (2 ounces)
   unsweetened chocolate,
   melted
1½ cups flour
½ teaspoon baking powder
¼ teaspoon salt

For the topping:
½ cup apricot jam, warmed
   and strained and mixed with
   1 tablespoon brandy
2 squares (2 ounces) semi-
   sweet chocolate
1 square (1 ounce)
   unsweetened chocolate
candied cherries cut in half

1. Cream the butter and sugar.
2. Add the egg yolk, vanilla and milk and blend well.
3. Add the melted chocolate and blend well.
4. Stir together the flour, baking powder and salt. Add to the creamed mixture and blend well. Refrigerate for 1 hour or until firm.
5. Shape the dough into a log about 1½–2 inches in diameter. Wrap it snugly in plastic and refrigerate for another 2–3 hours or until very firm.
6. Unwrap the dough and cut slices ¼ inch thick. Place the slices on the cookie sheet, leaving 1 inch between slices.
7. Bake for 10 minutes. Let the cookies cool slightly on the cookie sheet and then transfer carefully to wire racks to finish cooling.
8. Prepare the melted chocolate as described below. Then put the toppings on each cookie: Spread a little warm jam first; drizzle a little melted chocolate over the jam; finally, center half a candied cherry on the chocolate.

Preparing the chocolate

Melt the squares of chocolate in a heavy saucepan over low heat, stirring. When the chocolate is almost melted, turn off the heat and stir until it is completely melted. Add ½ tablespoon of warm water and stir well. The chocolate will get quite thick and somewhat tight. Add another

½ tablespoon of water and stir briskly; the chocolate will begin to thin out. Add 3 more tablespoons of water, ½ tablespoon at a time, stirring after each addition, to dilute the chocolate sufficiently to be drizzled. Less water will, of course, yield a thicker mixture.

Delia's Brownies

My dear friend Delia Ephron gave me this brownie recipe many years ago when we were both fledgling cooks. Recipes come and go but this one, like Delia, has never let me down.

Makes 16 brownies
Baking pan: 8″ × 8″, greased and floured
Preheat oven to 325°

2 squares (2 ounces) unsweetened chocolate
¼ cup butter
1 cup sugar
2 eggs, beaten
1 teaspoon vanilla
½ cup flour
pinch of salt
½ cup finely chopped walnuts or pecans

1. Melt the chocolate and butter in a heavy saucepan over very low heat, stirring constantly. Remove from the heat.

2. Add the sugar, mix well and let the mixture cool.

3. Add the eggs and vanilla and blend well.

4. Add the flour and salt and blend well by hand.

5. Stir in the nuts and spread the dough evenly in the pan.

6. Bake for 30–35 minutes. Place the pan on a wire rack and let the brownies cool in the pan. Cut into squares and remove carefully.

Mocha Fingers with Chocolate Sprinkles

Make these cookies with a cookie press or pastry bag fitted with a star tip (that's what makes the narrow ridges). The ends of each cookie are dipped in melted chocolate and chocolate sprinkles—sinfully rich but utterly delicious. Try the cookies with ice cream or sherbet.

Makes about 7½ dozen
   cookies
Baking pan: ungreased cookie
   sheet
Preheat oven to 350°

1 cup butter
¾ cup sugar
1 egg
1½ teaspoons vanilla
2 tablespoons strong coffee
2¼ cups flour
1 tablespoon unsweetened
   cocoa (not cocoa mix)
½ teaspoon baking powder
¼ teaspoon salt
3 squares (3 ounces) semi-
   sweet chocolate
chocolate sprinkles

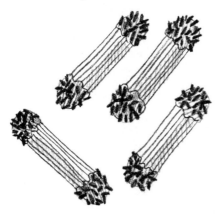

1. Cream the butter and sugar.
2. Add the egg, vanilla and coffee and blend well.
3. Stir together the flour, cocoa, baking powder and salt. Add gradually to the creamed mixture and blend well.
4. Pack half the dough (or less) at a time into a cookie press fitted with a small star disk or a pastry bag fitted with a large star tip. Press the dough onto the cookie sheet in 3-inch lengths, leaving 1 inch between cookies.
5. Bake for 5 minutes. Let the cookies cool on the cookie sheet for a minute or two and then transfer carefully to wire racks to finish cooling.
6. Prepare the semi-sweet chocolate for dipping, as described below, and put it into a small bowl. Put the chocolate sprinkles into another small bowl. Dip the ends of each cookie first in chocolate and then in sprinkles. Place on a wire rack while the chocolate hardens.

Preparing the chocolate

Melt the squares of chocolate in a heavy saucepan over very low heat, stirring. When the chocolate is almost melted, turn off the heat and stir until it is completely melted. Add ½ tablespoon of warm water and stir well. The chocolate will get quite thick and somewhat tight. Add another ½ tablespoon of water and stir briskly; the chocolate will begin to thin out. Add 3 more tablespoons of water, ½ tablespoon at a time, stirring after each addition, to thin the chocolate sufficiently for dipping. Less water will, of course, yield a thicker consistency.

Chocolate Chocolate Chip Cookies

Is this gilding the lily? Perhaps, but most chocolate lovers just can't get enough of their favorite flavor. These craggy little nuggets should please everyone—they're quick and easy to bake and they are certainly super-chocolatey.

Makes about 3 dozen cookies
Baking pan: greased cookie sheet
Preheat oven to 350°

¾ cup butter
1½ cups sugar
1 egg
1½ teaspoons vanilla
3 squares (3 ounces) unsweetened chocolate, melted
1¾ cups flour
¼ teaspoon salt
¾ cup (4½ ounces) chocolate chips
¾ cup chopped pecans

1. Cream the butter and sugar.
2. Add the egg and vanilla and blend well.
3. Add the melted chocolate and blend well.
4. Stir together the flour and salt. Add to the creamed mixture and blend well.
5. Stir in the chocolate chips and chopped pecans.
6. Drop the dough by rounded teaspoons onto the cookie sheet, leaving 1½ inches between drops.
7. Bake for 10 minutes. Watch carefully to be sure the bottoms don't burn; the cookies should be slightly soft in the center when they come out of the oven. Let them cool on the cookie sheet for 5 minutes and then transfer to wire racks to finish cooling.

Rum Truffles

Dense, dark and unrelentingly chocolatey, a confection worthy of a chocolate lover's complete attention. Store the truffles (carefully wrapped) in the refrigerator, but be sure to let them come to room temperature before serving so you can appreciate the full chocolate flavor.

Makes about 2½ dozen
   candies

6 squares (6 ounces)
   unsweetened chocolate
2 tablespoons butter
1 tablespoon heavy cream
6 tablespoons dark rum
2 egg yolks
2 cups sifted confectioners'
   sugar
unsweetened cocoa (not cocoa
   mix)

1. Melt the chocolate and butter in a heavy saucepan over low heat, stirring constantly. Remove from the heat.

2. Add the cream and rum and blend well.

3. Add the egg yolks and blend well.

4. Add the confectioners' sugar and stir. Knead with your hands until the mixture is smooth. Refrigerate for half an hour.

5. Dust your hands with confectioners' sugar. Shape the dough into balls about 1 inch in diameter. Roll each ball in a small bowl of cocoa. Refrigerate until ½ hour before serving. The truffles taste best at room temperature.

More chocolate cookies to make:
Mountain Tops, page 32
Devil's Food Cakes with Cream Filling,
   page 114

Spiced Chocolate Drops, page 33
Chocolate Shortbread Hearts,
   page 161

5. When Only Crunch Will Do: NUT COOKIES

Almond Meringues
Three Kinds of Nut Cups
   Almond Cherry Cups
   Walnut Raisin Cups
   Coconut Pecan Cups
Pecan Shortbread

Mixed-Up Nut Drops
Hazelnut Mounds
Cashew Cookies
Apricot Almond Cookies
Pistachio Logs

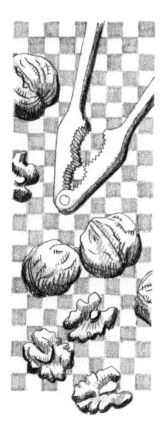

When it comes to flavor, texture and variety, you can't beat nut cookies. I think you'll find that this chapter has some of the most unusual and delicious nut cookie recipes you've ever tried. Nuts are equally delectable in a simple cookie like Mixed-Up Nut Drops or an elegant one like Almond Meringues with Mocha Glaze. They combine well with other flavors in Almond Cherry, Walnut Raisin and Coconut Pecan Nut Cups or stand invitingly alone in Pistachio Logs.

Above all, when cooking with nuts, learn to taste the difference between fresh nuts and stale ones. Because nuts are so rich in oil, the flavor can change drastically over time—especially if the nuts have been stored in a warm place. Unless you use them at a great rate, it's better to buy only small amounts of nuts, store them in the refrigerator and replenish them frequently from a market that regularly restocks its supply.

Almond Meringues

You might call this cookie a candy. It is crisp, crunchy and absolutely melting, with a bittersweet mocha glaze to offset the intense sweetness of the meringue. Use up all the dough in one baking (egg whites won't wait for tomorrow) by preparing two cookie sheets and putting them in the oven at the same time. Use half the dough on each sheet, about 24 cookies per sheet. They'll be close to each other and may even run together a bit, but they will taste just as good. Reminder: These are wonderful treats for folks who can't eat flour.

Makes about 4 dozen cookies
Baking pan: 2 greased and
   floured cookie sheets
Preheat oven to 250°

5 egg whites
2 pinches cream of tartar
2 pinches salt
½ teaspoon vanilla
¼ teaspoon almond extract
1¼ cups sugar
¾ cup ground almonds
¾ cup chopped almonds

Mocha Glaze (page 166)

1. Put the egg whites, cream of tartar, salt, vanilla and almond extract in a deep bowl. Beat until the egg whites hold soft peaks.

2. Add the sugar, one tablespoon at a time, while continuing to beat the egg whites. Beat until the mixture holds stiff peaks and all the sugar is dissolved.

3. Fold in the ground and chopped almonds.

4. Drop small mounds of meringue (about the size of Ping-Pong balls) on the two cookie sheets, leaving ½–1 inch between them. Try to fit 24 drops of meringue on each sheet. I use two spoons for making the mounds: one to scoop up the meringue from the bowl and the other to push it off and shape it.

5. The meringues must first bake and then dry in the oven: Bake the meringues for 40 minutes. Then turn off the heat and leave the meringues in the oven for 4–5 hours or overnight. Do not open the oven door during the entire drying time.

Carefully remove the meringues from the cookie sheet.

6. Place the meringues on a piece of waxed paper. Drizzle Mocha Glaze on the tops or simply dip the top of each meringue into a small bowl of Mocha Glaze. Let the glaze harden.

Three Kinds of Nut Cups

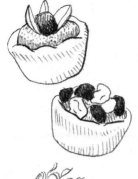

These pretty little cups are made from one basic dough plus your choice of three different fillings. Try them all— rich Almond Cherry, tart Walnut Raisin or crunchy Coconut Pecan. The flaky dough, made with cream cheese, is not sweet, so it provides a perfect counterpoint to the sweetness of the fillings.

Note: A gem muffin pan is simply a miniature muffin pan, with cups measuring almost 2 inches across the top.

Basic Dough

Whichever kind of cup you want to make, first prepare the Basic Dough according to this recipe. Then proceed to the filling of your choice and follow the steps carefully.

Makes 2 dozen nut cups
Baking pan: gem muffin pan,
ungreased

½ cup butter, softened
**1 3-ounce package of cream
cheese, softened**
1 cup flour

1. Cream the butter and cream cheese.
2. Add the flour and blend well. Divide the dough in half, wrap each half snugly in plastic and refrigerate for 2 hours.
3. Take one package of dough at a time out of the refrigerator. Divide the package of dough into 12 balls of equal size. Press a ball into each muffin cup, lining the bottom and sides evenly with dough. (When you complete the first batch of nut cups and the pan becomes available again, take out the second package of dough and repeat the process.)

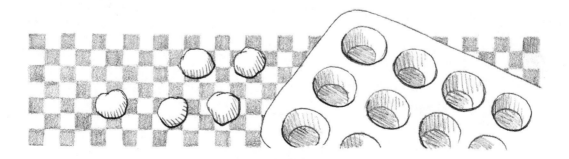

Almond Cherry Cups

Makes 2 dozen nut cups
Preheat oven to 400°

½ cup sugar
¼ cup almond paste
2 egg yolks
3 tablespoons flour
3 tablespoons milk
⅔ cup cherry preserves
   Note: Take the whole
     cherries out of the ⅔ cup
     jam, chop them up and
     stir them back into the
     jam.
24 additional cherries from the
   preserves
slivered toasted almonds

1. Combine the sugar and almond paste.
2. Add the egg yolks and beat well.
3. Add the flour and blend well.
4. Add the milk and blend well.
5. Put a scant teaspoon of cherry preserves in each prepared dough cup in the gem muffin pan. Put a rounded teaspoon of almond paste mixture on the preserves in each cup.
6. Bake for 15–20 minutes. The tops should be very lightly browned. Allow the cups to cool and then remove from the gem pan.
7. Take the second package of dough out of the refrigerator and line the cups of the gem muffin pan with dough as explained on page 61. Repeat steps 5 and 6, using the remaining half of the cherry preserves and almond paste mixture.
8. Top each cup with one cherry and a few slivered almonds.

Walnut Raisin Cups

Makes 2 dozen nut cups
Preheat oven to 400°

4 teaspoons honey
3 tablespoons sugar
½ cup orange juice
3 tablespoons water
scant teaspoon grated lemon
   rind
¾ teaspoon cinnamon
4 teaspoons flour
1 cup raisins
pinch of salt
½ cup chopped walnuts
½ teaspoon vanilla

1. Bake the unfilled dough cups for 10–12 minutes. Set them aside to cool. When they are cool, remove them from the pan. Take the second package of dough out of the refrigerator and line the cups of the gem muffin pan with dough as explained on page 61. Bake, set aside to cool and then remove from the pan.
2. Combine all ingredients except walnuts and vanilla in a heavy saucepan. Simmer, stirring constantly, for 5 minutes. Remove from the heat.
3. Add the walnuts and vanilla and blend well. Let the mixture cool.
4. Fill the dough cups with the walnut raisin mixture.

Coconut Pecan Cups

Makes 2 dozen nut cups
Preheat oven to 350°

4 tablespoons butter
4 tablespoons heavy cream
1¼ cups chopped pecans
¾ cup brown sugar
1 egg, beaten
1 teaspoon vanilla
pinch of salt
¼ cup sweetened flaked
    coconut
extra coconut for decoration

1. Put the butter and cream in a saucepan and bring just to a boil to melt the butter. Remove from the heat.

2. Stir in all the remaining ingredients except the extra coconut. Allow the mixture to cool and then divide in half.

3. Divide one half of the nut mixture equally among the 12 prepared dough cups in the gem muffin pan.

4. Bake the filled cups for 15–20 minutes. Allow them to cool in the pan and then remove carefully. Top each one with a sprinkle of coconut.

5. Take the second package of dough out of the refrigerator and line the cups of the gem muffin pan with dough as explained on page 61. Repeat steps 3 and 4, using the remaining half of the nut mixture.

Pecan Shortbread

Shortbread is one of the best and simplest cookies to make. Bake the shortbread until lightly browned around the edges—the pecans will smell toasty.

Makes 25 squares
Baking pan: 9" × 9", greased
    and floured
Preheat oven to 325°

½ cup butter
⅔ cup brown sugar
1 egg yolk
½ teaspoon vanilla
1¼ cups flour
pinch of salt
⅔ cup chopped pecans

1. Cream the butter and brown sugar.

2. Add the egg yolk and vanilla and blend well.

3. Stir together the flour, salt and pecans. Add to the creamed mixture and blend well.

4. Spread the dough evenly in the pan.

5. Bake for 25–30 minutes. The edges should be lightly browned and the tops should feel solid and not soft. Let the shortbread cool in the pan and then cut into small squares.

Mixed-up Nut Drops

This crisp, round cookie has a good brown sugar taste and an unusual free-for-all combination of mixed nuts. In fact, you can use up any nuts you have left over from other cooking projects. Be sure the ones you use are fresh; nothing ruins the flavor of a cookie faster than stale nuts.

Makes about 4½ dozen
  cookies
Baking pan: greased cookie
  sheet
Preheat oven to 325°

½ cup butter
½ cup margarine
2 cups brown sugar
2 eggs
1 teaspoon vanilla
2½ cups flour
½ teaspoon baking soda
¼ teaspoon salt
1½ cups chopped, mixed,
  unsalted nuts: walnuts,
  almonds, pecans, hazelnuts,
  cashews, peanuts

1. Cream the butter, margarine and brown sugar.

2. Add the eggs and vanilla and blend well.

3. Stir together the flour, baking soda, salt and chopped nuts. Add to the creamed mixture and blend well.

4. Drop the dough by rounded teaspoons onto the cookie sheet, leaving 2 inches between drops.

5. Bake for 15 minutes. Let the cookies cool on the cookie sheet for a minute or two and then transfer to wire racks to finish cooling.

Hazelnut Mounds

Crisp on the outside, tender on the inside—you almost have to pop the whole cookie into your mouth at one time. I suggest that you hold your hand under your chin while you eat because the cookie will crumble all over and you won't want to lose a single delicious bit. I enjoy them especially in the afternoon with a cup of tea or even a glass of sherry.

Makes about 4 dozen cookies
Baking pan: greased cookie
    sheet
Preheat oven to 325°

1 cup butter or ½ cup butter
    plus ½ cup margarine,
    softened
¼ cup sugar
¼ teaspoon salt
2 teaspoons vanilla
2 cups flour
2½ cups finely chopped
    toasted hazelnuts (see
    toasting directions below)
½ cup superfine sugar
2 egg whites slightly beaten
    with 2 teaspoons water

1. Mix together the butter, sugar, salt and vanilla.

2. Add the flour and 2 cups of the chopped hazelnuts and blend well. Refrigerate the dough for 3 hours or until firm enough to handle.

3. Dust your hands with flour, break off pieces of dough and shape balls about 1 inch in diameter.

4. In a small bowl stir together the remaining ½ cup of chopped hazelnuts and the superfine sugar. Brush each ball of dough with egg white and roll it in the nuts and sugar mixture. Place the balls on the cookie sheet about 1 inch apart.

5. Bake for 15–20 minutes, until lightly browned. Do not overbake. Cool on the cookie sheet for a few minutes and then transfer to wire racks to finish cooling.

Toasted hazelnuts

Preheat the oven to 300°. Place whole nuts on a baking sheet or pan and leave the nuts in the oven for 7 minutes or until the skins crack open and the nuts smell toasty.

Cashew Cookies

This cookie is distantly related to the peanut butter cookie but it has a mellow cashew taste you'll love. Don't flatten the cookies too much; they should be slightly thick with a crisp crumb. Watch them carefully toward the end of the baking period so the bottoms don't burn.

Makes about 3 dozen cookies
Baking pan: greased cookie
    sheet
Preheat oven to 375°

½ cup butter
½ cup sugar
½ cup brown sugar
1 egg
½ teaspoon vanilla
2 cups flour
¾ teaspoon baking soda
½ teaspoon salt
¼ teaspoon cinnamon
1 cup finely chopped unsalted
    cashews
cashew halves

1. Cream the butter, sugar and brown sugar.
2. Add the egg and vanilla and blend well.
3. Stir together the flour, baking soda, salt, cinnamon and chopped cashews. Add to the creamed mixture and blend well.
4. Drop the dough by rounded teaspoons onto the cookie sheet, leaving 1 inch between drops. Flatten each drop with a fork dipped in flour. Press half a cashew into the top of each cookie.
5. Bake for 8–10 minutes. Keep your eye on the cookies to be sure the bottoms don't burn. Let the cookies cool slightly on the cookie sheet and then transfer to wire racks to finish cooling.

Apricot Almond Cookies

A generous amount of chopped apricots and chopped almonds is mixed into the dough of these attractive rolled cookies. The apricots are chewy, the almonds are crunchy and the cookie itself is somewhere between soft and crisp.

Makes about 3 dozen cookies
Baking pan: greased cookie
   sheet
Preheat oven to 350°

2 cups flour
1 teaspoon baking powder
pinch of salt
6 tablespoons cold butter
⅓ cup sugar
⅓ cup brown sugar
1 egg
3 tablespoons milk
1 teaspoon vanilla
½ cup finely chopped dried
   apricots
½ cup finely chopped almonds

1. Stir together the flour, baking powder and salt.

2. Add the butter and cut it into the flour mixture with your fingers, a pastry cutter or a food processor. The texture should be crumblike.

3. Stir the sugar and brown sugar into the flour mixture.

4. Stir together the egg, milk and vanilla. Add to the flour mixture and blend well.

5. Stir in the apricots and almonds. Divide the dough in half, wrap each half snugly in plastic and refrigerate for 1–2 hours or until firm enough to roll out.

6. Dust the work surface and rolling pin with flour. Roll out half the dough at a time to about ⅛ inch thick. Cut rounds with a cookie cutter 1½–2 inches in diameter. Use a spatula to transfer the rounds to the cookie sheet, leaving 1 inch between them. Gather up the excess dough and save it for re-rolling.

7. Bake for 10 minutes. Cool the cookies on the cookie sheet for a minute and then transfer to wire racks to finish cooling.

Pistachio Logs

Shelling pistachio nuts is not the most thrilling way to spend an hour, even when you eat one nut for every two you put in the bowl. However, I promise that there will be a truly worthwhile reward for your trouble because these cookies are incredibly crisp, rich and elegant. They actually melt in your mouth.

Makes about 3 dozen cookies
Baking pan: ungreased cookie
   sheet
Preheat oven to 325°

1 cup butter, room temperature
¾ cup sugar
1 teaspoon vanilla
2½ cups flour
¼ teaspoon salt
½ cup ground pistachio nuts
confectioners' sugar

1. Cream the butter, sugar and vanilla.

2. Stir together the flour, salt and ground pistachio nuts. Add to the creamed mixture and blend well.

3. Break off a bit of dough and shape it into a little log about 2 inches long, ¾ inch wide and about ½ inch thick. Place the log on the cookie sheet. Repeat until all the dough is used, leaving 1½ inches between logs on the cookie sheet.

4. Bake for 15–20 minutes. The cookies should be slightly browned around the edges. They will be soft to the touch but will firm up as they cool. Let them cool on the cookie sheet for about a minute and then transfer to wire racks. While the logs are still warm, sprinkle them with confectioners' sugar sifted through a fine strainer.

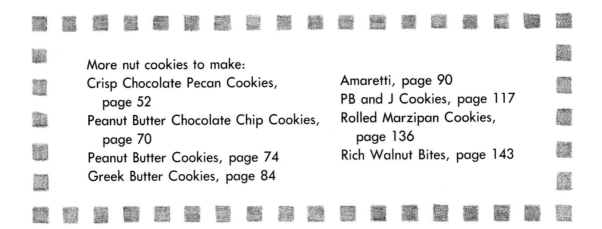

More nut cookies to make:
Crisp Chocolate Pecan Cookies,
   page 52
Peanut Butter Chocolate Chip Cookies,
   page 70
Peanut Butter Cookies, page 74
Greek Butter Cookies, page 84

Amaretti, page 90
PB and J Cookies, page 117
Rolled Marzipan Cookies,
   page 136
Rich Walnut Bites, page 143

6. Plain and Simple Comfort: FAVORITE COOKIES

Chocolate Chip Cookies
Peanut Butter Chocolate Chip Cookies
Oatmeal Raisin Drops
Coconut Cookies
Ginger Snaps
Peanut Butter Cookies
Big Sugar Cookies

Sand Bars
Turtles
Raisin Cookies
Refrigerator Cookies
Pressed Cookies
Butter Cookies
Jelly Tots

There are moments in a cookie lover's life when all the fancy lace wafers, ground hazelnut balls and chocolate shortbread in the world just won't make her happy. When all she really wants is a plain cookie: An oatmeal cookie. A raisin cookie. A coconut cookie. With milk.

This chapter is for those moments.

Chocolate Chip Cookies

What's left to be said about the nation's most popular cookie? Not a thing, except—try the recipe variation for Peanut Butter Chocolate Chip Cookies.

Makes about 3½ dozen
  cookies
Baking pan: greased cookie
  sheet
Preheat oven to 350°

½ cup butter
6 tablespoons sugar
6 tablespoons brown sugar
1 egg
1 teaspoon vanilla
1 cup flour
½ teaspoon baking soda
½ teaspoon salt
¾ cup (4½ ounces) chocolate
  chips
¾ cup coarsely chopped
  walnuts

1. Cream the butter, sugar and brown sugar.
2. Add the egg and vanilla and blend well.
3. Stir together the flour, baking soda and salt. Add to the creamed mixture and blend well.
4. Stir in the chocolate chips and chopped nuts.
5. Drop the dough by teaspoons onto the cookie sheet, leaving 2 inches between drops.
6. Bake for 10 minutes. Let the cookies cool on the cookie sheet for a minute or two and then transfer to wire racks to finish cooling.

Peanut Butter Chocolate Chip Cookies

6 tablespoons butter
¼ cup sugar
½ cup brown sugar
1 egg
1 teaspoon vanilla
2 tablespoons smooth peanut
  butter
1 cup flour
½ teaspoon baking soda
½ teaspoon salt
¾ cup (4½ ounces) chocolate chips
½ cup coarsely chopped walnuts
¼ cup coarsely chopped peanuts

Follow the same steps as for Chocolate Chip Cookies, adding the peanut butter when you add the egg and vanilla.

Oatmeal Raisin Drops

Thick in the middle, thin and crisp on the edges—the perfect oatmeal raisin cookie. Be sure the oats you use are the old-fashioned (not the quick-cooking) kind.

Makes about 3 dozen cookies
Baking pan: greased cookie
   sheet
Preheat oven to 350°

¾ cup margarine
½ cup sugar
¾ cup brown sugar
1 egg
¼ cup water
1 teaspoon vanilla
1 cup flour
2½ cups oatmeal (not the
   quick-cooking kind)
½ teaspoon baking soda
½ teaspoon salt
1 teaspoon cinnamon
1 cup raisins

1. Cream the margarine, sugar and brown sugar.

2. Add the egg, water and vanilla and blend well.

3. Stir together the flour, oatmeal, baking soda, salt, cinnamon and raisins. Add to the creamed mixture and blend well.

4. Drop the dough by rounded teaspoons onto the cookie sheet, leaving 2 inches between drops.

5. Bake for 10 minutes. Let the cookies cool on the cookie sheet for a minute or two and then transfer to wire racks to finish cooling.

Coconut Cookies

By toasting the coconut and adding a little coconut extract to the dough, you can turn out a cookie with a deliciously mellow but unmistakably coconutty flavor. The toasted coconut does great things for the texture of the cookie, too.

Makes about 2½ dozen
  cookies
Baking pan: ungreased cookie
  sheet
Preheat oven to 400°

½ cup butter
½ cup sugar
2 eggs
1 tablespoon milk
1 teaspoon vanilla
1 teaspoon coconut extract
2 cups flour
1½ teaspoons baking powder
¼ teaspoon salt
1 cup sweetened flaked or
  shredded coconut, toasted
  (see toasting directions
  below)

1. Cream the butter and sugar.
2. Add the eggs, milk, vanilla and coconut extract and blend well.
3. Stir together the flour, baking powder, salt and toasted coconut. Add to the creamed mixture and blend well.
4. Drop the dough by rounded teaspoons onto the cookie sheet, leaving 2 inches between drops. Using a glass with a flat bottom, dipped in flour, flatten each spoonful of dough to about ⅛-inch thick.
5. Bake for 5–8 minutes. Let the cookies cool slightly on the cookie sheet and then transfer to wire racks to finish cooling.

Toasted coconut

Place flaked or shredded coconut on an ungreased cookie sheet and bake in a 350° oven for 5–10 minutes, until lightly browned. Watch the coconut carefully, stirring it around once or twice.

Ginger Snaps

A ginger snap should be crisp on the outside and just a bit chewy on the inside, with an attractively crackled top. These fill the bill admirably. For a pleasant change, try spreading Milk Glaze on the tops—it softens the cookies and lightens the spice taste.

Makes about 4½ dozen
    cookies
Baking pan: greased cookie
    sheet
Preheat oven to 325°

6 tablespoons butter
½ cup sugar
½ cup brown sugar
1 egg
½ teaspoon vanilla
¼ cup molasses
2 cups flour
1 teaspoon baking soda
1 teaspoon ginger
½ teaspoon cinnamon
¼ teaspoon ground cloves

1. Cream the butter, sugar and brown sugar.

2. Add the egg, vanilla and molasses and blend well.

3. Stir together the flour, baking soda and spices. Add to the creamed mixture and blend well. Refrigerate the dough for 1 hour.

4. Shape the dough into balls about ¾ inch in diameter. Place the balls on the cookie sheet, leaving 1 inch between them.

5. Bake for 12–15 minutes. The cookies will puff up but will soon flatten out, get darker and show some crackling on top. Let the cookies cool slightly on the cookie sheet and then transfer to wire racks to finish cooling.

Variation

Spread the top of each cookie with Milk Glaze (page 165) and press a couple of raisins into the glaze.

Peanut Butter Cookies

Brown sugar and plenty of peanut butter make these cookies extra tasty. Of course they have the traditional criss-cross tops made with a fork, plus a couple of peanut halves pressed onto each cookie for good measure.

Makes about 3½ dozen cookies
Baking pan: greased cookie sheet
Preheat oven to 350°

½ cup butter or margarine
¾ cup smooth peanut butter
½ cup sugar
½ cup brown sugar
1 egg
½ teaspoon vanilla
1¼ cups flour
½ teaspoon baking soda
½ teaspoon salt
peanut halves, unsalted

1. Blend the butter and peanut butter.
2. Add the sugar and brown sugar and blend well.
3. Add the egg and vanilla and blend well.
4. Stir together the flour, baking soda and salt. Add to the peanut butter mixture and blend well.
5. Drop the dough by teaspoons onto the cookie sheet, leaving 1½ inches between drops. Flatten each cookie with a fork (dipped in flour, if necessary), pressing it into the cookie in both directions as shown in the drawing. Press two peanut halves into the top of each cookie.
6. Bake for 15 minutes. The cookies should be slightly browned and just beginning to get firm to the touch. Allow the cookies to cool on the cookie sheet for a few minutes and then transfer to wire racks to finish cooling.

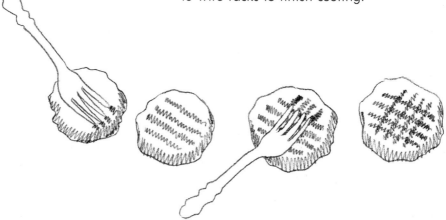

Big Sugar Cookies

If you can eat only one of these big cookies and then push the plate away, you have more will power than I do. They're good any way you make them—plain, sprinkled with cinnamon sugar or spread with glaze.

Makes about 3 dozen cookies
Baking pan: greased cookie sheet
Preheat oven to 350°

¾ cup butter
¾ cup margarine
1 cup sugar
2 eggs
1½ teaspoons vanilla
1 tablespoon grated lemon rind
3¾ cups flour
1 teaspoon baking powder
½ teaspoon salt
1 egg white mixed with
   1 teaspoon water
sugar

1. Cream the butter, margarine and sugar.

2. Add the eggs, vanilla and grated lemon rind and blend well.

3. Stir together the flour, baking powder and salt. Add to the creamed mixture and blend well. Divide the dough in half, wrap each half snugly in plastic and refrigerate for several hours or until firm enough to roll out.

4. Dust the work surface and rolling pin with flour. Roll out half the dough at a time to ⅛-inch thick. Cut with a large cookie cutter. Gather up the excess dough and save it for re-rolling. With a spatula, transfer the cookies to the cookie sheet.

5. Brush each cookie with egg white and sprinkle with sugar.

6. Bake for 8 minutes, until golden. Let the cookies cool slightly on the cookie sheet and then transfer to wire racks to finish cooling.

Variations

1. Cut the cookies with heart, spade, club and diamond cookie cutters.

2. Brush the unbaked cookies with egg white and sprinkle with colored sugar or cinnamon sugar instead of plain sugar.

3. Spread the baked cookies with Mocha Glaze (page 166) or Milk Glaze (page 165).

Sand Bars

These cookies are thin, crisp and as sweet as a confection. You will certainly want to try the variations, which lift the cookie to astonishing heights. Variation #1 creates a delightful counterpoint between sweet and semi-sweet; variation #2 is the one for chocoholics; variation #3 is so good you'll eat too many of them.

Makes about 4 dozen cookies
Baking pan: ungreased cookie sheet
Preheat oven to 400°

½ cup butter
1¼ cups sugar
1 egg
1 teaspoon vanilla
¼ teaspoon almond extract
2 cups flour
¼ teaspoon salt

1. Cream the butter and sugar.
2. Add the egg, vanilla and almond extract and blend well.
3. Stir together the flour and salt. Add to the creamed mixture and blend well. Divide the dough in half, wrap each half snugly in plastic and refrigerate for 1 hour or until firm enough to roll out.
4. Dust the work surface and rolling pin with flour. Roll out half the dough at a time to a rectangle about ⅛-inch thick. Cut the dough in 1 × 2¾-inch bars. Carefully transfer the bars to the cookie sheet, leaving 1 inch between them. Gather up and save the excess dough for re-rolling.
5. Bake for 6 minutes or until the edges are slightly browned. Watch carefully to be sure the cookies don't burn. Let the cookies cool on the cookie sheet for only a minute or two and then transfer to wire racks to finish cooling.

Variations

1. Melt squares of semi-sweet chocolate. Dip or paint the ends of each bar in melted chocolate. Set the bars on wire racks while the chocolate hardens.
2. Dip (or paint) the ends of the bars in melted chocolate and then in chocolate sprinkles.
3. Dip the ends of the bars in warm apricot jam and then in chocolate sprinkles.

Turtles

Another cookie straight from your childhood—soft, tasty and silly-looking. They're easy and fun to make, but be careful not to let the turtles' pecan feet burn. Brush the melted chocolate onto the cookies with a flat, ½-inch wide brush.

Makes about 3 dozen cookies
Baking pan: ungreased cookie sheet
Preheat oven to 350°

¾ cup margarine
⅔ cup brown sugar
1 egg
1½ teaspoons vanilla
1¾ cups flour
1 teaspoon baking powder
¼ teaspoon salt
pecan halves
¾ cup (4½ ounces) chocolate chips

1. Cream the margarine and brown sugar.
2. Add the egg and vanilla and blend well.
3. Stir together the flour, baking powder and salt. Add to the creamed mixture and blend well. Refrigerate the dough for 2 hours or until firm.
4. To make each cookie, first arrange 5 pecan halves on the cookie sheet as shown in the drawing. Next dampen your hands and shape a ball of dough about 1–1½ inches in diameter. Press the ball onto the pecan halves. Continue making cookies, leaving 1 inch between them.
5. Bake for 15 minutes. Allow the cookies to cool slightly on the cookie sheet and then transfer to wire racks to finish cooling.
6. Melt the chocolate chips in the top of a double boiler and keep the chocolate warm. Use a flat brush to spread melted chocolate on the top of each cookie. Take care not to get chocolate on the pecans.

Raisin Cookies

These are big, soft cookies with crisp edges, loaded with plump raisins and crunchy walnuts, tasting faintly of nutmeg and cinnamon. Like all drop cookies, they are quick and easy to make, so you can keep the cookie jar chock-full.

Makes about 3 dozen cookies
Baking pan: greased cookie sheet
Preheat oven to 350°

½ cup butter
½ cup sugar
½ cup brown sugar
2 eggs
¼ cup milk
1 teaspoon vanilla
2 cups flour
1 teaspoon baking powder
½ teaspoon salt
1 teaspoon cinnamon
½ teaspoon nutmeg
1 cup raisins
¾ cup chopped walnuts

1. Cream the butter, sugar and brown sugar.
2. Add the eggs, milk and vanilla and blend well.
3. Stir together the flour, baking powder, salt, spices, raisins and nuts. Add to the creamed mixture and blend well.
4. Drop the dough by rounded teaspoons onto the cookie sheet, leaving 2 inches between drops. Flatten each cookie slightly with a fork or spoon dipped first in flour.
5. Bake for 10–12 minutes. Transfer the cookies to wire racks to cool.

Refrigerator Cookies

When I was a child in the 1950s, these cookies were called icebox cookies. Iceboxes were already a thing of the past and refrigerators had arrived to stay, but the name of the cookies hadn't yet caught up with the technology. The cookies remained the same, though—conveniently sliced from a chilled log of dough, popped in the oven at a moment's notice, delicious any time.

Makes about 4 dozen cookies

Baking pan: greased cookie sheet

Preheat oven to 350°

¾ cup butter or margarine
½ cup sugar
½ cup brown sugar
1 egg
1½ teaspoons vanilla
2 cups flour
½ teaspoon baking powder
¼ teaspoon salt
½ teaspoon nutmeg

1. Cream the butter, sugar and brown sugar.
2. Add the egg and vanilla and blend well.
3. Stir together the flour, baking powder, salt and nutmeg. Add to the creamed mixture and blend well. Refrigerate the dough for 3 hours or until firm.
4. Dust your hands with flour and shape the dough into a log about 2 inches in diameter. Wrap snugly in plastic and refrigerate until very firm.
5. Unwrap the dough and cut slices ⅛-inch thick. Place the slices on the cookie sheet, leaving 2 inches between them. You do not have to slice all the dough at one time; slice as many cookies as you need and refrigerate or freeze the remaining dough for future use.
6. Bake for 10 minutes, until lightly browned. The cookies will be a little soft on top when they come out of the oven, but they will get crisp as they cool. Let the cookies cool for a minute or two on the cookie sheet and then transfer to wire racks to finish cooling.

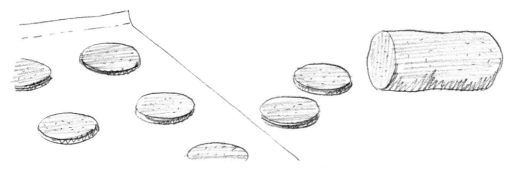

Pressed Cookies

For this recipe you will need either a cookie press or a pastry bag to pipe the dough into the traditional S-shapes. The baked result is a fragile, delicate cookie with that perfectly simple taste you get only from a combination of butter, sugar, egg yolk and vanilla.

Makes about 1½ dozen
  cookies
Baking pan: ungreased cookie
  sheet
Preheat oven to 350°

1 cup butter, room temperature
½ cup superfine sugar
1 egg yolk
1 teaspoon vanilla
1¾ cups flour
pinch of salt

1. Cream the butter and superfine sugar.
2. Add the egg yolk and vanilla and blend well.
3. Add the flour and salt and blend well. Divide the dough in half, cover each half snugly with plastic and refrigerate for 1 hour.
4. Fit a cookie press with a small star disk or fit a pastry bag with a large star tip. Spoon half the dough at a time into the cookie press or pastry bag. Pipe S-shapes directly onto the cookie sheet, leaving 2 inches between cookies, following the drawing for guidance. Cover the cookie sheet lightly with plastic wrap and refrigerate for 1 hour to set the shapes.
5. Bake for 10 minutes. Let the cookies cool on the cookie sheet for a minute or two and then transfer carefully to wire racks to finish cooling.

Butter Cookies and Jelly Tots

This is another recipe from my grandmother, Blanche Small. She uses it to make either round, flat butter cookies or small jelly tots—cookies with jelly- or jam-filled craters in the center.

Butter Cookies

Makes about 3½ dozen
  cookies
Baking pan: greased cookie
  sheet
Preheat oven to 375°

¾ cup butter
½ cup sugar
1 egg plus one egg yolk
1 teaspoon vanilla
½ teaspoon grated lemon rind
  (optional)
1½ cups sifted flour
½ teaspoon salt

1. Cream the butter and sugar.
2. Add the egg, egg yolk, vanilla and lemon rind (if desired) and blend well.
3. Stir together the flour and salt. Add to the creamed mixture and blend well. Chill the dough for 2 hours or until firm.
4. Dust your hands with flour and shape the dough into balls about 1 inch in diameter. Place the balls on the cookie sheet, leaving 2 inches between them. Using a glass with a flat bottom, dipped in flour, gently flatten each ball to ⅛-inch thick.
5. Bake the cookies for 12 minutes or until the edges are brown. Let the cookies cool slightly on the cookie sheet and then transfer to wire racks to finish cooling.

Jelly Tots

Makes about 3 dozen cookies

The ingredients are the same with two exceptions: Increase the amount of sifted flour to 1¾ cups; have on hand some of your favorite jam or jelly.

Follow steps **1**, **2** and **3** on page 81.

4. Dust your hands with flour and shape the dough into balls 1 inch in diameter. Place the balls 1½ inches apart on the cookie sheet.

5. Bake for 5 minutes. Take the cookie sheet out of the oven and use a thimble to make a depression in the center of each cookie.

6. Return the cookie sheet to the oven and bake for 8–10 more minutes or until lightly browned around the edges. Let the cookies cool slightly on the cookie sheet and then transfer to wire racks to finish cooling.

7. When the cookies are cool, fill the depressions with jelly or jam.

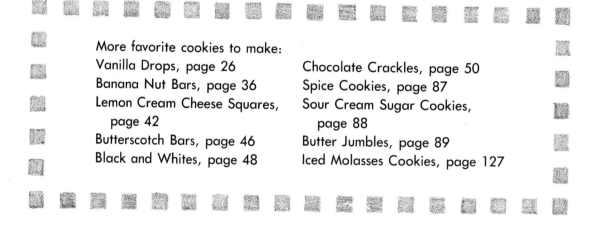

7. A Taste of Love and Tradition: GRANDMA'S COOKIES

Greek Butter Cookies
Mexican Cookies
Simple Stars
Spice Cookies
Sour Cream Sugar Cookies
Butter Jumbles
Amaretti

Italian Sesame Cookies
Rich Cookies with Poppy Seeds
    or Poppy Seed Filling
Scotch Shortbread
Shortcut Rugelach
Flaky Hungarian Cookies with Jam

These recipes have their origins all over the world—Greece, Mexico, Scotland, Germany, Hungary, Italy. This is especially appropriate for a book of great American cookies, since many of us are the children or grandchildren of immigrants who brought with them their particular styles of cooking and favorite recipes—and passed them along to us.

So we are blessed with cookie recipes and more cookie recipes, of which only a few fit into this one chapter. But even these few remind us how important (and delicious) it is to preserve our traditional recipes.

These recipes may be very different from your own family favorites, but in the American spirit of sharing our traditions, I hope you'll add them to your repertoire.

Greek Butter Cookies

Another one of those nutty little round cookies that actually melts in your mouth. Because there is very little sugar in the cookie dough, the finished cookies do need that extra sprinkling of confectioners' sugar at the end—so don't be tempted to skip that step.

Makes about 3½ dozen
 cookies
Baking pan: ungreased cookie
 sheet
Preheat oven to 325°

1 cup butter, softened
6 tablespoons sifted
 confectioners' sugar
1 egg yolk
½ teaspoon vanilla
½ teaspoon almond extract
½ cup finely chopped toasted
 almonds (see toasting
 directions below)
2–2¼ cups flour
½ teaspoon baking powder

1. Cream the butter until fluffy. Add the sifted confectioners' sugar and cream again.

2. Add the egg yolk, vanilla and almond extract and blend well.

3. Add the chopped almonds and blend well.

4. Stir together 2 cups of the flour and the baking powder and work into the creamed mixture to get a dough that is soft but not too sticky. Add the additional ¼ cup of flour if necessary. Chill the dough for 30 minutes or until firm.

5. Shape the dough in balls about 1 inch in diameter. Place the balls on the cookie sheet and flatten slightly.

6. Bake for 20 minutes. Sprinkle with confectioners' sugar sifted through a fine strainer. Let the cookies cool on the cookie sheet.

Toasted almonds

Preheat the oven to 300°. Spread whole almonds (blanched or with the skins) on a cookie sheet and leave them in the oven for 10–15 minutes, stirring the nuts often. They are done when they have a toasty smell and taste; blanched almonds will look toasted, too.

Mexican Cookies

You will be pleasantly surprised by the combination of cinnamon, cloves and orange in these very special cookies. They come out of the oven rather soft, but as they cool they harden to a dense, crisp texture.

Makes about 2–3 dozen
  cookies
Baking pan: greased cookie
  sheet
Preheat oven to 375°

½ cup margarine
½ cup plus 2 tablespoons
  sugar
1 egg, beaten
2 teaspoons grated orange rind
3 tablespoons orange juice
2⅓ cups flour
pinch of salt
½ teaspoon cinnamon
¼ teaspoon ground cloves
⅓ cup finely chopped pecans
confectioners' sugar

1. Cream the margarine and sugar.

2. Add the egg, grated orange rind and orange juice and blend well.

3. Stir together the flour, salt and spices. Add to the creamed mixture and blend well.

4. Stir in the chopped pecans. Divide the dough in half, wrap each half snugly in plastic and refrigerate for 1 hour or until firm enough to roll out.

5. Dust the work surface and rolling pin with flour. Roll out half the dough at a time to ⅛-inch thick. Cut with cookie cutters. Lift away the excess dough and save it for re-rolling. Transfer the cookies to the cookie sheet, leaving 1 inch between them.

6. Bake for 12–15 minutes. Allow the cookies to cool slightly on the cookie sheet and then transfer to wire racks. While the cookies are still warm, sprinkle with confectioners' sugar sifted through a fine strainer.

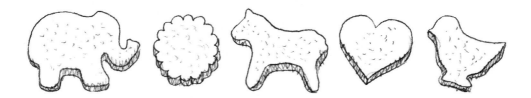

Simple Stars

Although my mother, Claire Javna, became a grandma only recently, these cookies of hers are definitely a taste of love and tradition. The dough is quite easy to work with and produces a thin, crisp, melting cookie that goes exceptionally well with milk after school.

Makes about 2½ dozen
  cookies
Baking pan: greased cookie
  sheet
Preheat oven to 375°

½ cup butter
1 cup sugar
2 egg yolks
1 tablespoon heavy cream
½ teaspoon vanilla
1½ cups flour
1 teaspoon baking powder
½ teaspoon salt
30 or more blanched almonds
2 egg whites
2 tablespoons sugar mixed
  with ½ teaspoon cinnamon

1. Cream the butter and sugar.

2. Add the egg yolks, cream and vanilla and blend well.

3. Stir together the flour, baking powder and salt. Add to the creamed mixture and blend well. Divide the dough in half, wrap each half snugly in plastic and refrigerate for 3 hours or until firm enough to roll out.

4. Dust the work surface and rolling pin with flour and roll out half the dough at a time to ⅛-inch thick. Cut with a 3-inch-wide star cookie cutter. Lift away the excess dough and save it for re-rolling. Transfer the stars to the cookie sheet.

5. Press an almond into the center of each cookie. Brush each cookie with egg white and sprinkle with the mixture of sugar and cinnamon.

6. Bake for 8 minutes. Let the cookies cool on the cookie sheet for a minute or two and then transfer carefully to wire racks to finish cooling.

Spice Cookies

Here's a rich but not overwhelming molasses and spice cookie. It's thin and toasty—a perfect match for a crisp apple on a fall day.

Makes about 3½ dozen
   cookies
Baking pan: greased cookie
   sheet
Preheat oven to 375°

1 cup margarine
½ cup molasses
6 tablespoons brown sugar
2½ cups flour
½ teaspoon baking soda
½ teaspoon salt
½ teaspoon cinnamon
½ teaspoon ground cloves
1 teaspoon ginger

1. Melt the margarine in a saucepan. Add the molasses and brown sugar and stir over low heat until the sugar dissolves. Pour the mixture into a mixing bowl and let it cool.

2. Stir together the flour, baking soda, salt and spices. Add to the melted sugar mixture and blend well. Divide the dough in half, wrap or cover each half snugly with plastic and refrigerate overnight to ripen.

3. Dust the work surface and rolling pin generously with flour and roll out half the dough at a time to ⅛-inch thick. Cut with cookie cutters. Lift up the excess dough and save it for re-rolling. Transfer the cookies to the cookie sheet.

4. Bake for 10 minutes. Let the cookies cool slightly on the cookie sheet and then transfer to wire racks to finish cooling.

Variation

Spread a little Rum Glaze (page 166) on each cookie and top with a bit of candied orange peel.

Sour Cream Sugar Cookies

This is a good basic sugar cookie with the added attraction of half a cup of sour cream in the dough. The flavor, crispness and colored sugar decoration make me think of bakery cookies—or the way bakery cookies would taste and look if they were as good as homemade.

Makes about 2½ dozen
   cookies
Baking pan: greased cookie
   sheet
Preheat oven to 375°

¼ cup butter
1 cup sugar
½ teaspoon baking soda
½ cup sour cream
1 egg plus 1 egg yolk
½ tablespoon grated lemon
   rind
½ teaspoon vanilla
2½ cups flour
½ teaspoon salt
1 egg white mixed with 1½
   teaspoons water
colored sugar or colored dots

1. Cream the butter and sugar.
2. Stir the baking soda into the sour cream. Add to the creamed mixture and blend well.
3. Add the egg, egg yolk, grated lemon rind and vanilla and blend well.
4. Stir together the flour and salt. Add to the creamed mixture and blend well. Divide the dough in half, wrap each half snugly in plastic wrap and refrigerate for 3 hours or until firm enough to roll out.
5. Dust the work surface and rolling pin with flour. Roll out half the dough at a time to ⅛-inch thick. Cut with large cookie cutters. Lift away the excess dough and save it for re-rolling.
6. Brush the tops of the cookies with egg white and sprinkle with colored sugar or colored dots. Transfer the cookies to the cookie sheet.
7. Bake for 12 minutes. Transfer the cookies to wire racks to cool.

Butter Jumbles

Butter Jumbles are simple, old-fashioned cookies. This recipe comes from my grandmother, Blanche Small. If you make the criss-cross indentations firmly, the tops will bake to a pretty combination of pale tan and warm toast.

Makes about 5 dozen cookies
Baking pan: greased cookie sheet
Preheat oven to 425°

1 cup butter
1¾ cups confectioners' sugar
2½–3 cups flour
pinch of salt
¼ cup water (approximately)

1. Cream the butter and confectioners' sugar.

2. Stir the salt into the flour. With your hands, work 2½ cups of the flour into the creamed mixture alternately with small amounts of water. The dough is ready when your hands come out clean, which may require using that extra ½ cup flour.

3. Shape the dough into walnut-size balls and place the balls on the cookie sheet, leaving 1½ inches between them. Using a fork dipped in flour, make criss-cross indentations on each cookie as shown in the drawing.

4. Bake for 10 minutes. The edges should be brown. Let the cookies cool on the cookie sheet for a minute or two and then transfer to wire racks to finish cooling.

Amaretti

Crisp on the outside, chewy on the inside—just the way an almond macaroon should be. For gift-giving or for parties, wrap each cookie in a 7-inch square of tissue paper and twist the paper closed as shown in the drawing.

Makes about 7 dozen cookies
Baking pan: greased and
  floured cookie sheet
Preheat oven to 275°

3 egg whites
1 tablespoon Amaretto liqueur
  or 1 teaspoon almond extract
3 cups blanched almonds,
  ground
1½ cups sugar
2 pinches salt
confectioners' sugar

1. Beat the egg whites until they are stiff but not dry. Beat in the liqueur or almond extract.

2. Stir together the ground almonds, sugar and salt. Fold into the egg whites.

3. Drop the dough by teaspoons onto the cookie sheet, leaving 1 inch between drops.

4. Sprinkle the dough lightly with confectioners' sugar sifted through a fine strainer.

5. Bake for 25 minutes or until golden on the edges. Remove the cookies to wire racks to cool.

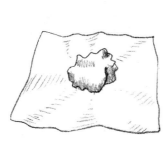

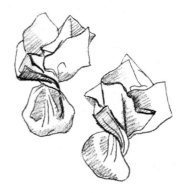

Italian Sesame Cookies

These might be called sweet biscuits instead of cookies. The flavor is mild, only slightly sweet, with the nutty taste of lots of sesame seeds; the texture is crumbly and only a little crisp. Delicious with a cup of tea or a glass of red wine.

Makes about 1½ dozen
  cookies
Baking pan: greased and
  floured cookie sheet
Preheat oven to 350°

½ cup butter
¼ cup sugar
¼ cup brown sugar
2 eggs
1 teaspoon vanilla
2 cups flour
2 teaspoons baking powder
¼ teaspoon salt
milk
½–¾ cup sesame seeds

1. Cream the butter, sugar and brown sugar.
2. Add the eggs and vanilla and blend well.
3. Stir together the flour, baking powder and salt. Add gradually to the creamed mixture, blending well.
4. Turn out the dough onto a floured surface and knead 1–2 minutes until the dough is smooth.
5. Break off a small piece of dough and roll it in your palms to make an oval about 2 inches long and ¾-inch thick. Dip the oval in milk and roll it in sesame seeds. Place the cookie on the cookie sheet. Repeat with the remaining dough.
6. Bake for 15 minutes or until golden. Remove the cookies to wire racks to cool.

Rich Cookies with Poppy Seeds or Poppy Seed Filling

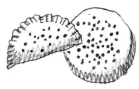

Make this recipe either as flat round cookies topped with a sprinkling of poppy seeds or as baby turnovers with poppy seed filling.

Makes about 2–2½ dozen
    cookies
Baking pan: greased and
    floured cookie sheet
Preheat oven to 350°

1 cup butter
⅔ cup sugar
2 hard-cooked egg yolks
1 egg yolk
1 teaspoon grated lemon rind
1½ teaspoons vanilla
2¼ cups flour
½ teaspoon salt
1 egg white mixed with 1
    teaspoon water
poppy seeds

Poppy Seed Filling (optional)

1. Cream the butter and sugar.

2. Sieve the hard-cooked egg yolks. Add them, along with the egg yolk, grated lemon rind and vanilla, to the creamed mixture and blend well.

3. Stir together the flour and salt. Add to the creamed mixture and blend well. Divide the dough in half, wrap each half snugly in plastic and refrigerate for 2 hours or until firm enough to roll out.

4. Dust the work surface and rolling pin with flour. Roll out half the dough at a time to ⅛-inch thick. Cut with a round cookie cutter about 3 inches in diameter. Lift away the excess dough and save it for re-rolling.

5. If you are making flat cookies with a sprinkling of poppy seeds, brush each round with egg white and sprinkle poppy seeds generously over the egg white. Transfer the cookies to the cookie sheet, leaving ½ inch between rounds.

If you are making turnovers with filling, put a teaspoon of Poppy Seed Filling in the center of each round. Carefully fold the dough over the filling and seal the turnover by crimping the edge firmly with a fork. Brush the top of each turnover with egg white and sprinkle lightly with poppy seeds. Prick the turnovers with the fork.

6. Bake the flat rounds for 10–12 minutes, until they are lightly browned. Bake the turnovers for 15–20 minutes, until they are lightly browned. Let the rounds and/or turnovers cool on the cookie sheet for a few minutes and then transfer to wire racks to finish cooling.

Poppy Seed Filling

Makes about 1¼ cups

1 cup poppy seeds
⅓ cup milk
2 tablespoons honey
1 tablespoon grated lemon rind
1 egg, beaten

Stir together the poppy seeds, milk, honey and lemon rind in a saucepan and simmer for about 10 minutes. Remove from the heat and allow the mixture to cool. Stir in the egg.

Scotch Shortbread

Jane Ross, my colleague in publishing, collected this traditional recipe many years ago. You may have to hunt a bit for rice flour, but it's well worth the search. Try Asian groceries, health food stores or gourmet food departments.

Makes about 2 dozen cookies
Baking pan: ungreased cookie
  sheet
Preheat oven to 400°

1 cup butter
½ cup sugar
2 cups flour
¾ cup rice flour

1. Cream the butter and sugar.
2. Gradually add the flour and the rice flour, working them in with your hands.
3. Pat the dough into a rectangle ¾-inch thick and 5 inches wide. Cut the rectangle into bars 2½ inches long and ¾-inch wide, as shown in the drawing. Prick the top of each bar with a fork.

Transfer the bars to the cookie sheet.
4. Bake for 8–10 minutes. The bars will puff up and get longer during baking. Transfer to wire racks to cool.

Shortcut Rugelach

I love this rugelach recipe because you can really taste all the different flavors—butter, cream cheese, apricot, raisins. The dough is soft, so working with it does take some patience, but the technique of rolling the dough on sugar-sprinkled wax paper helps things along.

Makes about 2–3 dozen
  cookies
Baking pan: greased cookie
  sheet
Preheat oven to 375°

½ cup butter
1 3-ounce package of cream
  cheese
⅓ cup sugar
1 egg
½ teaspoon vanilla
1 cup flour
1 cup cake flour
pinch of salt
⅔ cup apricot jam, warmed
1 cup raisins
1 cup finely chopped walnuts
1 tablespoon grated lemon rind
½ teaspoon cinnamon
¼ teaspoon nutmeg

1. Cream the butter, cream cheese and sugar.
2. Add the egg and vanilla and blend well.
3. Stir together the flour, cake flour and salt. Add to the creamed mixture and blend well to make a smooth dough. Refrigerate the dough for 2 hours or until firm enough to roll out.
4. Sprinkle sugar generously on a piece of waxed paper 18 inches long. Roll out the dough on the waxed paper to a rectangle about 10 × 12 inches. Using a pastry brush, carefully spread the warm jam on the dough.
5. Stir together the raisins, chopped walnuts, lemon rind and spices. Sprinkle evenly over the jam.
6. Roll up the dough from long edge to long edge, lifting the waxed paper to help you roll. Refrigerate the roll for half an hour.
7. Slice the roll in 1-inch-wide pieces. Cut each piece in half. Use a spatula to place the pieces on the cookie sheet, leaving 1½ inches between them.
8. Bake for 20–25 minutes. Let the rugelach cool on the cookie sheet for a minute or two and then transfer to wire racks to finish cooling.

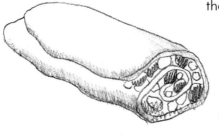

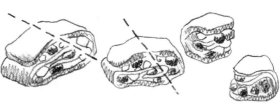

Flaky Hungarian Cookies with Jam

Many thanks to Kathy Sizemore for this recipe, which is as incredibly good as she promised it would be. The cookie is light, flaky and buttery and has no sugar in the dough; the only sweetness comes from the jam tucked into the cookie. Pay close attention to the rolling instructions, for therein lies the secret to the success of these cookies.

Makes about 5½ dozen
  cookies
Baking pan: ungreased cookie
  sheet
Preheat oven to 375°

4 cups sifted cake flour
1 teaspoon baking powder
1 cup cold water
1 tablespoon white vinegar
2 egg yolks
1 cup butter
1 cup margarine
2 tablespoons cake flour
jam (strawberry, apricot or
  raspberry are recommended)
confectioners' sugar

1. Stir together the 4 cups of cake flour and the baking powder.

2. Add the water, vinegar and egg yolks and mix with your hands until the dough comes cleanly off them. Refrigerate the dough until firm.

3. When the dough is firm, prepare the butter mixture: Combine the butter and margarine by mixing and mashing them together. Add the 2 tablespoons of cake flour and mash that in, too. The mixture should be soft, of spreading consistency. Between uses you may store the butter mixture in a cool spot instead of refrigerating it; this avoids having to mash it to softness each time you use it.

4. Dust the work surface and rolling pin with flour. Roll out the dough to ¼-inch thick. VERY IMPORTANT: When you roll out the dough, roll *either* away from you or toward you but *not* in both directions. Spread one quarter of the butter mixture evenly over the rolled dough. Fold the dough in half and then in quarters, as shown below.

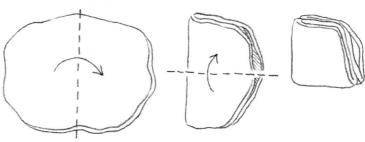

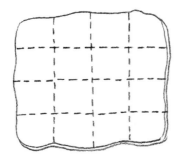

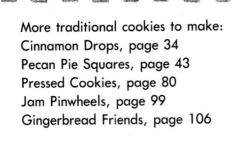

Wrap the dough in plastic and return it to the refrigerator for 6 hours. Repeat the process described on the preceding page (rolling out the dough, spreading it with butter mixture, folding in half and then in quarters) 3 more times. However, refrigerate just 3 hours between rollings.

5. Cut the dough in quarters. Wrap three of the quarters in plastic and return them to the refrigerator. Roll out the fourth piece of dough to a rectangle. Cut it in 2-inch squares, using a pastry cutting wheel or a sharp knife. Put a dab of jam in the middle of each square and fold opposite corners over the jam.

Transfer the cookies to the cookie sheet. Repeat the process described above (rolling out the dough, cutting it in squares, adding jam and folding the dough) with the remaining dough.

6. Bake for 15 minutes. The cookies are finished when the layers look flaky, puffed and golden. Transfer the cookies to wire racks to cool and then sprinkle with confectioners' sugar sifted through a fine strainer.

8. Especially for Children: COOKIE CUTTER COOKIES

Brown Sugar Bears
Jam Pinwheels
Funny Faces
Babies in Blankets
Snowfolks

Greeting Card Cookies
Gingerbread Friends
Fancy Cookies Made of Simple Shapes
Mittens and Gloves
Noah's Ark

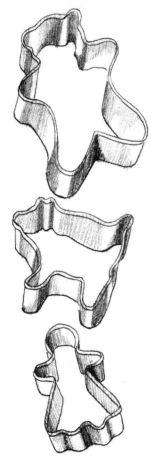

This is the chapter in which you really get to play with rolled cookie dough. There's a range of cookies from the basic, simple (and undecorated) Babies in Blankets and Jam Pinwheels to the more ambitious and jazzy Greeting Card Cookies, Noah's Ark and Funny Faces. And for Christmas, try Snowfolks and Gingerbread Friends.

Many of the cookies have decorations, but don't think you have to be an artist to do them. The pressed-on decorations (like raisins) are simply pushed directly into the dough or glaze or attached with a dab of egg white. The piped-on decorations (made of Decorating Icing) are applied with a pastry bag and icing tips or by a special super-easy, no-mess method using plastic bags (see pages 21–24 for extended instructions).

All the cookies can be made at least in part by children, with some adult supervision. For example, children may need some help rolling out the dough, but try to let them do as much as they can. Of course, you can make these cookies all by yourself—you'll have just as good a time cutting and decorating as any child could.

Brown Sugar Bears

These crisp, toasty bears have a delightful brown sugar taste that everyone will love. They require very little decoration so even the most junior member of the household can put the finishing touches on a bear—a pair of raisins or nuts for eyes and perhaps a few more for paws.

Makes about 3 dozen cookies
Baking pan: greased cookie
   sheet
Preheat oven to 400°

½ cup butter
1 cup dark brown sugar
1 egg
2½ cups flour
1 teaspoon baking powder
½ teaspoon salt
1 teaspoon vanilla
¼ cup milk

For decorating:
raisins, broken nuts, assorted
   small candies of your choice

1. Cream the butter and light brown sugar.
2. Add the egg and blend well.
3. Stir together the flour, baking powder and salt.
4. Stir the vanilla into the milk. Add to the creamed mixture alternately with the dry ingredients. Blend well after each addition. Divide the dough in half, wrap each half snugly in plastic and refrigerate for 2 hours or until firm enough to roll out.
5. Dust the work surface and rolling pin with flour. Roll out half the dough at a time to ⅛-inch thick. Use a teddy bear cookie cutter (mine measures 2¼ × 3¼ inches) to cut as many bears as you can. Lift away the excess dough and save it for re-rolling. With a spatula, transfer the bears to the cookie sheet, leaving ½ inch between them.
6. Decorate each bear with raisins, nuts or candies, pressing the decorations firmly into the cookies.
7. Bake for 8–12 minutes. Allow the cookies to cool on the cookie sheet for a minute or two and then transfer to wire racks to finish cooling.

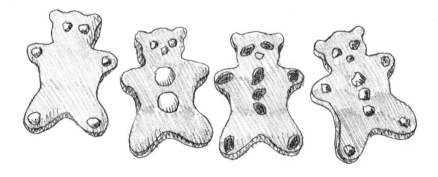

Jam Pinwheels

This is a buttery, almost flaky cookie with a dab of jam in the middle. They're fun to make, and the sugar you sprinkle over the pinwheels after baking covers up any cracks and flaws in the fragile dough.

Makes about 2½ dozen
  cookies
Baking pan: greased and
  floured cookie sheet
Preheat oven to 350°

1 cup butter
⅔ cup sugar
1 egg
1½ teaspoons vanilla
2½ tablespoons water
3 cups flour
1 teaspoon baking powder
2 pinches of salt
jam
sugar

1. Cream the butter and sugar.
2. Add the egg, vanilla and water and blend well.
3. Stir together the flour, baking powder and salt. Add to the creamed mixture and blend well. Divide the dough in quarters, wrap each quarter snugly in plastic and refrigerate for 1½ hours or until firm enough to roll out.
4. Dust the work surface and rolling pin with flour. Roll out one package of dough at a time to a rectangle about ⅛-inch thick and 6 inches wide. Cut the dough into 3-inch squares. (A fluted pastry wheel works very well for this job.) Transfer the squares to the cookie sheet, leaving 1 inch between them.
5. Make cuts in each square as shown in the drawing. Put a small spoonful of jam in the center of one square and spread it around a bit with the back of the spoon. Fold the four points of the square over the jam to make a pinwheel and press the points down in the center of the cookie. Repeat with all the squares.
6. Bake for 12–15 minutes. Sprinkle the hot cookies with sugar. Let the cookies cool slightly on the cookie sheet and then transfer carefully to wire racks to finish cooling.

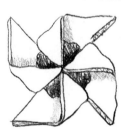

Funny Faces

There is no end to the number of silly things you can do to a Funny Face cookie. You can stick little pieces of dough on the cookie to make eyes, nose, lips and ears. You can force dough through a garlic press and attach it to make hair and a beard. You can sprinkle colored sugars, colored dots or colored candies here and there. Check the drawings for ideas and then take off on your own. How about a self-portrait?

Makes about 2 dozen cookies
Baking pan: ungreased cookie
    sheet
Preheat oven to 375°

1 cup butter
1 cup sugar
1 teaspoon vanilla
2 tablespoons milk
2½ cups flour

For decorating:
egg white
chocolate chips, raisins,
    candied fruit, chopped and
    whole nuts, assorted small
    candies, colored sugars,
    sprinkles and dots

1. Cream the butter and sugar.

2. Add the vanilla and milk and blend well.

3. Add the flour gradually, beating well. As the dough gets stiffer, you might prefer to work in the remaining flour with your hands. Divide the dough in half, wrap each half in plastic and refrigerate for 2 hours or until firm enough to roll out.

4. Dust the work surface and rolling pin with flour. Roll out half the dough at a time to a little less than ¼-inch thick. Cut with a round cookie cutter about 3 inches in diameter. Gather up the excess dough and save it for re-rolling. Transfer the rounds to the cookie sheet, leaving only ½ inch between them.

5. Decorate the rounds to make the faces shown in the drawings or invent your own silly faces. Use bits of dough to make features and force dough through a garlic press to make hair, beards and moustaches. Attach all decorations with egg white, using your finger to apply the egg white to the cookie. Press raisins, nuts and other tidbits firmly into the cookies.

6. Bake for 8–10 minutes. Allow the cookies to cool slightly on the cookie sheet and then transfer to wire racks to finish cooling.

Babies in Blankets

Sarah Brennan's mom sent a box of these cookies to nursery school for Sarah's third birthday party, secretly doubting that kids would even look at cookies with apricots and prunes tucked inside. Oh, well, she thought philosophically, at least there'll be a few left over for Ed and me. Wrong again. Kids just love these cookies. There were none left over for Ed and Jane, and even Sarah's teacher had to sprint to nab one for herself.

Makes about 4½ dozen
   cookies
Baking pan: greased cookie
   sheet
Preheat oven to 350°

1 cup butter or margarine
⅔ cup sugar
1 egg
1½ teaspoons vanilla
3 cups flour
1 teaspoon baking powder
2 pinches of salt
1 tablespoon grated orange
   rind
dried apricots, cut in half
dried prunes, pitted and cut in
   half lengthwise

1. Cream the butter and sugar.
2. Add the egg and vanilla and blend well.
3. Stir together the flour, baking powder, salt and grated orange rind. Add to the creamed mixture and blend well. Divide the dough in half, wrap each half in plastic and refrigerate for 1 hour or until firm enough to roll out.
4. Plump the apricots and prunes by pouring hot water over them, adding a squeeze of lemon juice and allowing them to sit in the water for 20 minutes. Pour the water off and pat the fruit dry with paper towels.
5. Dust the work surface and rolling pin with flour and roll out half the dough at a time to ⅛-inch thick. Cut with a round or scalloped cookie cutter about 2½ inches in diameter. Gather up the excess dough and save it for re-rolling. Place a piece of apricot or prune in the center of each round and fold the dough over to wrap the "baby" in the "blanket," as shown in the drawing. Pinch the dough envelope to keep it from opening during baking. Transfer the cookies to the cookie sheet.
6. Bake for 12–15 minutes. Let the cookies cool on the cookie sheet for a minute or two and then transfer to wire racks to finish cooling.

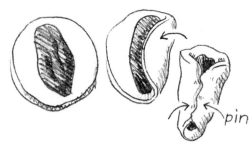

pinch

Snowfolks

Here is a light, soft gingerbread cookie for you to spread with Milk Glaze and decorate with chocolate chips, cinnamon redhots and drifts of shredded coconut.

Makes about 20 big cookies
   (each 4" × 3") and 3 dozen
   smaller cookies (each 3" ×
   2")
Baking pan: greased cookie
   sheet
Preheat oven to 325°

⅔ cup light brown sugar
½ cup dark corn syrup
1 teaspoon cinnamon
1 teaspoon ginger
½ teaspoon ground cloves
1½ teaspoons vanilla
½ teaspoon salt
2½ teaspoons baking soda
¾ cup margarine
1 egg
4 cups flour

Milk Glaze (page 165)

For decorating:
miniature chocolate chips,
   cinnamon redhots,
   sweetened shredded coconut

1. Combine the light brown sugar, corn syrup, spices, vanilla and salt in a heavy saucepan and bring to a boil, stirring continuously. Turn off the heat and stir in the baking soda.

2. Put the hot mixture in a bowl and add the margarine, stirring until it melts.

3. Add the egg and blend well.

4. Gradually add the flour and blend to make a smooth dough. Turn the dough out onto a floured surface and knead several times. Divide the dough in thirds, wrap each part snugly in plastic and refrigerate for 1 hour or until firm enough to roll out.

5. Dust the work surface and rolling pin with flour. Roll out one third of the dough at a time to a little less than ¼-inch thick. Cut with a large or small snowman cookie cutter or cut some of each size. Gather up the excess dough and save it for re-rolling. Transfer the snowfolks to the cookie sheet, leaving 1 inch between them.

6. Bake for 10–14 minutes. Let the cookies cool slightly on the cookie sheet and transfer to wire racks to finish cooling.

7. Spread or paint two cookies with Milk Glaze. While the glaze is still warm and soft, decorate each cookie with chocolate chips, redhots and/or coconut, pressing the decorations firmly into the glaze. Let the glaze harden. Repeat for as many cookies as you like.

Greeting Card Cookies

Use these large painted cookies to say Merry Christmas, Happy Birthday or Get Well Soon. The drawings will give you some decorating ideas to get you started. Notice the little shapes and strips of dough that are attached with egg white and baked onto the cookies.

Makes about 11 cookies
Baking pan: ungreased cookie
    sheet
Preheat oven to 375°

1 cup butter
1 cup sugar
1 teaspoon vanilla
2 tablespoons milk
2½ cups flour

For decorating:
1 egg white mixed with 1
    tablespoon water
chocolate chips, raisins,
    chopped or whole nuts,
    assorted small candies,
    colored sprinkles, chocolate
    sprinkles
food coloring

1. Cream the butter and sugar.
2. Add the vanilla and milk and blend well.
3. Add the flour gradually, beating well. As the dough gets stiffer, you may find it easier to work in the flour with your hands. Divide the dough in half, wrap each half snugly in plastic and refrigerate for 2 hours or until firm enough to roll out.
4. Dust the work surface and rolling pin with flour. Roll out half the dough at a time to a little less than ¼-inch thick. To make each basic card, cut a 4 × 6-inch rectangle. (A 4 × 6-inch index card makes a good template for cutting and a fluted pastry wheel gives a pretty edge.) To make the dough decorations for each card, cut at least one small cookie cutter shape like a heart, star or miniature boy or girl, plus a couple of narrow strips of dough if you like. Check the drawings for guidance.
    Transfer the dough rectangles to the cookie sheet, leaving ½ inch between them.
5. Paint egg white on each rectangle and arrange the small shapes and strips of dough in a pleasing design. Add chocolate chips, raisins or other small tidbits to make a border decoration, pressing each bit firmly into the dough. Be sure to leave a clear central space for painting your message, as shown in the drawings.
6. Bake for 10 minutes. Let the cookies cool slightly on the cookie sheet and then transfer to wire racks to finish cooling.

7. When the cookies are cool, paint your greeting in the clear spaces, using an artist's brush and food coloring slightly diluted with water. You may also want to paint colors on the attached shapes. If you have no brushes handy, use cotton swabs for painting.

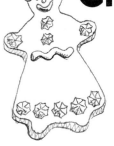

Gingerbread Friends

No cookie book would be complete without gingerbread boys and girls, and this recipe makes dozens of the best gingerbread cookies I've ever tasted. Decorate with piped icing in a variety of pastel colors, using the no-mess method explained in detail on pages 23–24.

Makes about 40 big cookies (each 5" × 3½") or 100 smaller cookies (each 2" × 1½")

Baking pan: ungreased cookie sheet

Preheat oven to 350°

½ cup margarine
½ cup dark brown sugar
½ cup molasses
1 egg
2½ cups flour
1½ teaspoons baking soda
½ teaspoon salt
1½ teaspoons cinnamon
1 teaspoon ginger
½ teaspoon ground cloves

Decorating Icing (page 21)
food coloring

1. Cream the margarine, dark brown sugar and molasses.

2. Add the egg and blend well.

3. Stir together the flour, baking soda, salt and spices. Add to the creamed mixture and blend well. If the dough seems too sticky, add a little more flour. If the dough is difficult to blend with a spoon, you may prefer to work the flour in with your hands. Divide the dough in half, wrap each half snugly in plastic and refrigerate for 2 hours or until firm enough to roll out.

4. Dust the work surface and rolling pin with flour. Roll out half the dough at a time to ¼-inch thick. Cut big and/or small people with cookie cutters. Gather up the excess dough and save it for re-rolling. Transfer the cookies to the cookie sheet.

5. Bake for 6–8 minutes. Allow the cookies to cool slightly on the cookie sheet and then transfer to wire racks to finish cooling.

6. Decorate the cooled cookies with Decorating Icing piped through a pastry bag or an ordinary food storage plastic bag; read pages 21–24 for complete instructions on both methods, as well as information about coloring the icing.

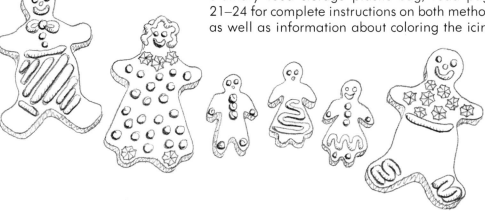

Fancy Cookies Made of Simple Shapes

A little imagination is all it takes to turn even the most basic shapes into fancy cookies. The drawings below will give you lots of ideas and inspiration.

Here's how to do it: Roll out some chilled dough to ¼-inch thick (try the Brown Sugar Bears dough). Cut out the components with cookie cutters, a knife or even a drinking glass. Rearrange the pieces to make the fancy shapes and "glue" them together with a little egg white. (Be sure to pat and push the pieces together firmly so they do not separate during baking.) Use a spatula to transfer the cookies to cookie sheets, decorate if you like and then bake.

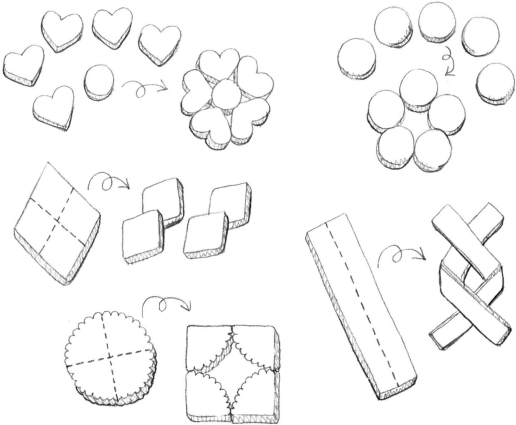

Mittens and Gloves

No ready-made cookie cutter required for this big cookie—all you need is a hand and a dull knife. The decorations are a simple sprinkling of colored sugar plus lots of little goodies pressed right into the dough.

Makes about 18 cookies
Baking pan: greased cookie
   sheet
Preheat oven to 375°

¾ cup butter
1 cup sugar
2 egg yolks
¼ cup orange juice
1 teaspoon vanilla
2⅓ cups flour
1 teaspoon baking powder
½ teaspoon salt

For decorating:
2 egg whites mixed with 1
   teaspoon water
colored crystal sugar
colored dots, raisins, chocolate
   chips, assorted small
   candies, imperials, peanut
   halves

1. Cream the butter and sugar.

2. Add the egg yolks, orange juice and vanilla and blend well.

3. Stir together the flour, baking powder and salt. Add to the creamed mixture and blend well to make a smooth dough. Divide the dough in half, wrap the halves snugly in plastic and refrigerate for 1 hour or until firm enough to roll out.

4. Dust the work surface and rolling pin generously with flour and roll out half the dough at a time to a little less than ¼-inch thick. To make each cookie, flour your child's hand, place it on the dough and cut around it with a dull knife. The drawing below shows how to cut a mitten (without fingers) or a glove (with fingers). Cut the dough straight across at the wrist. Lift away the excess dough and save it for re-rolling. Transfer the cookies to the cookie sheets, leaving 1 inch between them.

5. Decorate the cookies before baking but while they are sitting on the cookie sheet. Paint each glove and mitten with egg white and sprinkle with colored crystal sugar. Blow away the excess sugar. Add raisins, nuts and candies, pressing each one firmly into the dough. The drawings will give you some ideas.

6. Bake for 10–12 minutes. Let the cookies cool slightly on the cookie sheet and then transfer to wire racks to finish cooling.

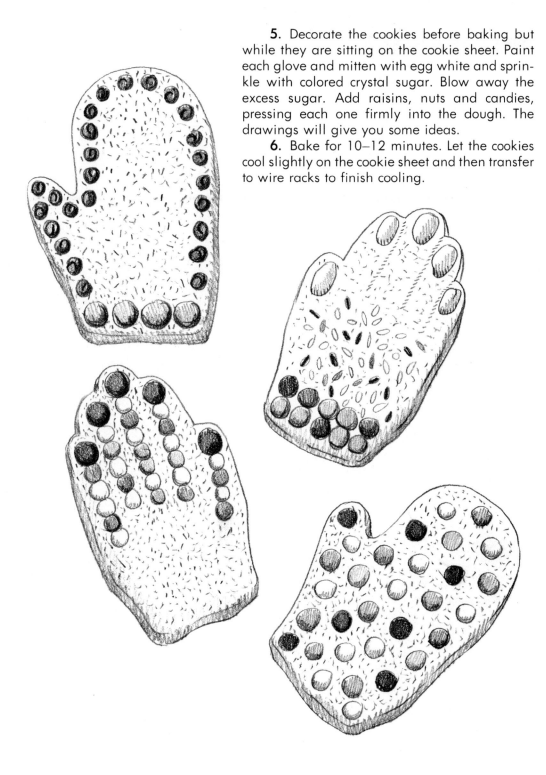

Noah's Ark

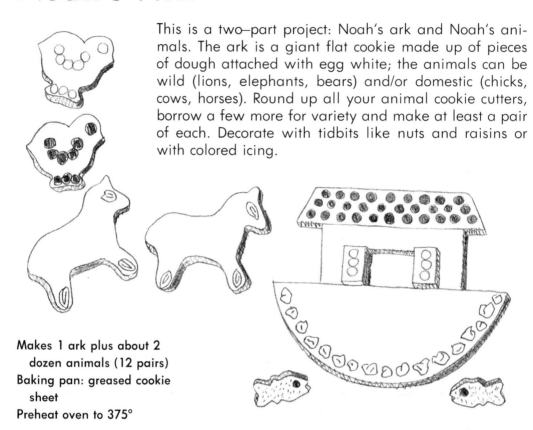

This is a two–part project: Noah's ark and Noah's animals. The ark is a giant flat cookie made up of pieces of dough attached with egg white; the animals can be wild (lions, elephants, bears) and/or domestic (chicks, cows, horses). Round up all your animal cookie cutters, borrow a few more for variety and make at least a pair of each. Decorate with tidbits like nuts and raisins or with colored icing.

Makes 1 ark plus about 2
   dozen animals (12 pairs)
Baking pan: greased cookie
   sheet
Preheat oven to 375°

½ cup butter
1 cup sugar
1 egg
1 tablespoon milk
1 teaspoon vanilla
2¼–2½ cups flour
1 teaspoon baking powder
½ teaspoon salt
1 egg white

For decorating:
raisins, currants, nuts,
   chocolate chips and other
   small candies
Decorating Icing (page 21)
food coloring

1. Cream the butter and sugar.
2. Add the egg, milk and vanilla and blend well.
3. Stir together 2¼ cups of the flour, the baking powder and salt. Add to the creamed mixture and blend well to make a smooth dough. If the dough seems too sticky, add the extra ¼ cup of flour. Divide the dough in half, wrap each half snugly in plastic and refrigerate for 2 hours or until firm enough to roll out.
4. Make the ark first: Dust the work surface and rolling pin generously with flour. Roll out half the dough to a little less than ¼-inch thick. Cut out the pieces of the ark as shown in the

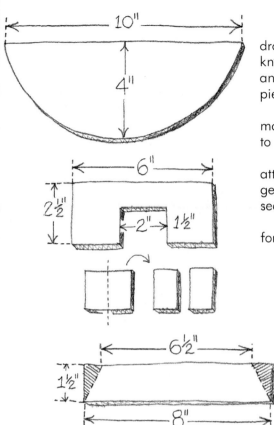

drawing. Use a dinner plate, ruler and sharp knife to make the semicircular piece; use a ruler and the same sharp knife to cut the other two pieces.

Cut the rectangular piece as shown, to make the opening. Cut the removed piece in half to make the doors and set them aside.

Transfer the pieces to the cookie sheet and attach them to each other with a little egg white, gently pressing the pieces together to join them securely. Now attach the doors with egg white.

Gather up the excess dough and save it for re-rolling.

5. There is probably room on the cookie sheet to fit some of the animal cookies, so go ahead and roll out all the remaining dough to ¼-inch thick and cut out pairs of animals. Fit as many cookies as possible on the cookie sheet with the ark, leaving 1 inch between cookies. The rest of the animals will be baked in second and third batches.

6. Before you bake the ark and the animals, decide how you will decorate them. If you wish to decorate with colored icings, bake first (step 7) and then pipe the icing on the cooled cookies (step 8). If you prefer to decorate the ark and the animals with raisins, nuts and candies, do so right now before baking. Follow the drawings for guidance and be sure to press these decorations firmly into the dough.

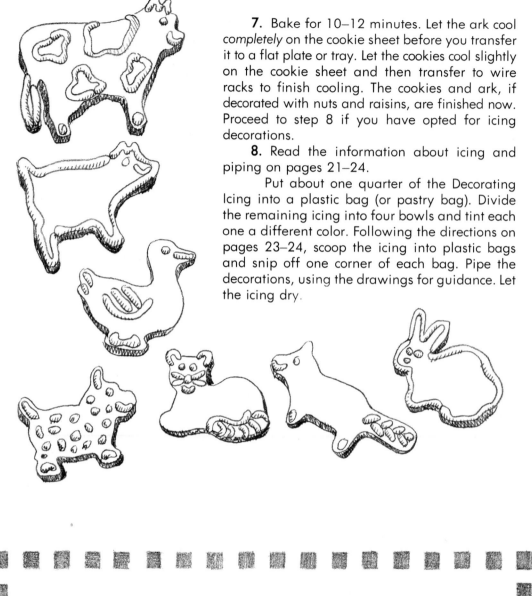

7. Bake for 10–12 minutes. Let the ark cool *completely* on the cookie sheet before you transfer it to a flat plate or tray. Let the cookies cool slightly on the cookie sheet and then transfer to wire racks to finish cooling. The cookies and ark, if decorated with nuts and raisins, are finished now. Proceed to step 8 if you have opted for icing decorations.

8. Read the information about icing and piping on pages 21–24.

Put about one quarter of the Decorating Icing into a plastic bag (or pastry bag). Divide the remaining icing into four bowls and tint each one a different color. Following the directions on pages 23–24, scoop the icing into plastic bags and snip off one corner of each bag. Pipe the decorations, using the drawings for guidance. Let the icing dry.

More cookie cutter cookies to make:
Chocolate Linzer Tarts, page 49   Gingerbread Angels, page 152
Big Sugar Cookies, page 75   Sugar Cookie Ornaments, page 159
Mexican Cookies, page 85   Cinnamon Sweethearts, page 160
Simple Stars, page 86   Linzer Hearts, page 162

9. Two Cookies Are Better Than One: SANDWICH COOKIES

Devil's Food Cakes with Cream Filling
Orange Marmalade Sandwiches
Fresh Fruit Pockets
PB and J Cookies
Butterscotch Sandwiches

Ginger Orange Sandwiches
Big Fig Sandwiches
Date, Nut and Cream Cheese
   Sandwiches

Sandwich cookies, like sandwiches, are a great American institution. Is there a cookie lover who hasn't carefully pried apart a cream-filled cookie, eaten the cookie that doesn't have the cream and then slowly nibbled the one that does?

Of course, the most interesting thing about a sandwich cookie is the filling. On the other hand, what's a filling without two delicious cookies to hold it? In this chapter you can take your choice of Ginger Orange or Big Fig Sandwiches, Devil's Food Cakes with Cream Filling or tasty little apple pies called Fresh Fruit Pockets.

Sandwich cookies are made like any other cookies, with two additional steps: making the filling and then sandwiching it between two cookies. The filling goes between the wrong sides of two cookies (the finished cookies have the right sides showing); be sure to brush the crumbs away from the wrong sides of the cookies before trying to spread the filling. And remember that you'll end up with half as many finished (filled) cookies as you have baked, so plan accordingly.

Devil's Food Cakes with Cream Filling

There are few kinds of cookies more generally beloved than this one. This version is a handful of soft, cakelike chocolate cookie with a buttery vanilla filling. The dough is rather soft and sticky so be sure to sprinkle flour generously on the work surface and the bottom of the glass used for flattening the cookies.

Makes about 2½ dozen
  sandwiches (5 dozen
  cookies)
Baking pan: ungreased cookie
  sheet
Preheat oven to 350°

1 cup butter or margarine
1½ cups sugar
2 eggs
2 teaspoons vanilla
2½ cups flour
½ cup unsweetened cocoa (not
  cocoa mix)
1½ teaspoons baking powder
½ teaspoon salt

Cream Filling

1. Cream the butter and sugar.
2. Add the eggs and vanilla and blend well.
3. Stir together the flour, cocoa, baking powder and salt. Add to the creamed mixture and blend well. Divide the dough into four parts, wrap each part snugly in plastic and refrigerate until firm.
4. Work with one package of dough at a time; the colder it is, the easier it is to work with. Break off pieces of dough and shape into balls about 1 inch in diameter. Place the balls on the cookie sheet, leaving 2 inches between them. Find a glass with a flat bottom, dust the bottom generously with flour and use it to flatten each ball to about ¼-inch thick.
5. Bake for 8 minutes, watching carefully to be sure the bottoms of the cookies don't burn. Let the cookies cool slightly on the cookie sheet and then transfer to wire racks to finish cooling.
6. Brush the crumbs off the wrong sides of the cookies. Spread Cream Filling on the wrong sides of half the cookies and cover with the remaining cookies.

Cream Filling

Makes about 1¼ cups

¼ cup butter, softened
3 teaspoons vanilla
3 tablespoons heavy cream
2½ cups confectioners' sugar

Stir all the ingredients together and beat until smooth and spreadable.

Orange Marmalade Sandwiches

The use of marmalade as a filling produces a most unusual and delicious sandwich. It's easy to make, too, since the cookie dough is dropped and then flattened with a glass instead of rolled and cut with a cookie cutter.

Makes about 2½ dozen
   sandwiches (5 dozen
   cookies)
Baking pan: greased and
   floured cookie sheet
Preheat oven to 350°

½ cup butter
½ cup margarine
1 cup sugar
1 egg
1 teaspoon vanilla
2 tablespoons lemon juice
2½ cups flour
½ teaspoon baking soda
½ teaspoon salt
1 tablespoon grated lemon rind
orange marmalade, warmed

1. Cream the butter, margarine and sugar.
2. Add the egg, vanilla and lemon juice and blend well.
3. Stir together the flour, baking soda, salt and grated lemon rind. Add to the creamed mixture and blend well.
4. Drop the dough by teaspoons onto the cookie sheets, leaving 2½ inches between drops. Find a glass with a flat bottom, dip the bottom in flour and use it to flatten each drop of dough to about ⅛-inch thick.
5. Bake for 8–10 minutes. Let the cookies cool slightly on the cookie sheet and then transfer to wire racks to finish cooling.
6. Brush the crumbs off the wrong sides of the cookies. Spread warm marmalade on the wrong sides of half the cookies and cover with the remaining cookies.

Fresh Fruit Pockets

This is an endearing cookie, something like a soft little pie with apple filling. The dough is quite buttery, so it needs a liberal amount of flour sprinkled on the work surface and rolling pin when you roll it out. You'll find that the extra flour will not harm the taste or texture of the cookie.

Makes about 3 dozen pockets
Baking pan: greased cookie
   sheet
Preheat oven to 350°

1 cup butter or margarine
¾ cup sugar
¾ cup light brown sugar
2 eggs
2 tablespoons milk
1 teaspoon vanilla
3¾ cups flour
1 teaspoon baking powder
1 teaspoon baking soda
½ teaspoon salt

Apple Filling

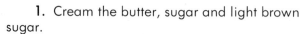

1. Cream the butter, sugar and light brown sugar.

2. Add the eggs, milk and vanilla and blend well.

3. Stir together the flour, baking powder, baking soda and salt. Add to the creamed mixture and blend well. Divide the dough in half, wrap each half snugly in plastic and refrigerate for 2 hours or until firm enough to roll out.

4. Dust the work surface and rolling pin generously with flour. Roll out half the dough at a time to ⅛-inch thick. Cut in rounds 2 inches in diameter or in 2-inch squares. Gather up the excess dough for re-rolling to make more rounds or squares. Transfer half the rounds (or squares) to the cookie sheet.

5. Put a teaspoon of filling in the center of each round on the cookie sheet. Cover with the remaining rounds. Place the cookie sheet in the refrigerator for 20 minutes to allow the dough to firm up. Crimp the edge of each pocket with a fork as shown in the drawings (the cooled dough will permit crisper, more attractive crimping). Prick each pocket with the points of the fork.

6. Bake for 10–15 minutes. Let the pockets cool on the cookie sheet for a minute or two and then transfer to wire racks to finish cooling.

Apple Filling

Makes about 2½ cups

4 Macintosh apples
1 tablespoon butter
½ cup raisins
2 tablespoons light brown
 sugar
1 teaspoon cinnamon
¼ teaspoon ginger
pinch of salt

Peel the apples and core them carefully, removing all the seeds and other hard matter from the center. Chop the apples into pieces about ¼-inch square.

Melt the butter in a saucepan. Add the apples, raisins, light brown sugar, spices and salt and cook, stirring, until the apples soften. Do not let the apples get mushy. Remove from the heat, drain off any liquid and allow the mixture to cool.

PB and J Cookies

A brand-new kind of peanut butter and jelly sandwich— this one is a pair of very peanutty peanut butter cookies with your favorite jam spread between them.

Makes about 2 dozen
 sandwiches (4 dozen
 cookies)
Baking pan: greased cookie
 sheet
Preheat oven to 375°

½ cup butter
½ cup sugar
½ cup brown sugar
1 egg
1 teaspoon vanilla
¾ cup chunky peanut butter
1½ cups flour
½ teaspoon baking soda
½ teaspoon salt
jam

1. Cream the butter, sugar and brown sugar.
2. Add the egg and vanilla and blend well.
3. Add the peanut butter and blend well.
4. Stir together the flour, baking soda and salt. Add to the creamed mixture and blend well. Refrigerate the dough for 1½ hours or until firm.
5. Dust your hands with flour. Break off bits of the dough and shape into balls about 1 inch in diameter. Place the balls on the cookie sheet, leaving 2 inches between them. Find a glass with a flat bottom, dip the bottom in flour and use it to flatten each ball to about ⅛-inch thick.
6. Bake for 7–10 minutes. Let the cookies cool slightly on the cookie sheet and then transfer to wire racks to finish cooling.
7. Brush the crumbs off the wrong sides of the cookies. Spread jam on the wrong sides of half the cookies and cover with the remaining cookies.

Butterscotch Sandwiches

This is the cookie for serious butterscotch lovers. Not only does the dough itself have that brown-sugary, butterscotch taste, but the filling is made with melted butterscotch chips. Keep the roll of dough in the freezer and slice off as many cookies as you need whenever the craving strikes.

Makes about 2½ dozen
    sandwiches (60 cookies)
Baking pan: greased cookie
    sheet
Preheat oven to 350°

½ cup butter
½ cup sugar
¼ cup light brown sugar
1 egg
1½ teaspoons vanilla
1¾ cups flour
½ teaspoon baking powder
¼ teaspoon salt
½ cup finely chopped almonds
    or pecans
butterscotch chips

1. Cream the butter, sugar and light brown sugar.

2. Add the egg and vanilla and blend well.

3. Stir together the flour, baking powder, salt and chopped nuts. Add to the creamed mixture and blend well. Refrigerate the dough for 45 minutes or until firm enough to handle.

4. Shape the dough into one or two logs 1½ inches in diameter. Wrap snugly in plastic and return to the refrigerator to firm up.

5. For each sandwich cut two ⅛-inch-thick slices from the log of dough. Place the slices ¾ inch apart on the cookie sheet. Cut a few extra slices and place them on the cookie sheet as well.

6. Bake for 10–12 minutes, until lightly browned on the edges. Let the cookies cool on the cookie sheet for a minute or two and then transfer to wire racks to finish cooling.

7. Turn half the cookies wrong side up on the cookie sheet. Place a few butterscotch chips in the center of each and cover with the remaining cookies. Put the sandwiches back into the hot oven for a minute or two to melt the butterscotch chips. Remove the sandwiches from the oven and press each one to spread the melted chips.

Ginger Orange Sandwiches

These spicy cookies are made with honey and molasses, and the creamy filling gets its real orange flavor from real grated orange rind. Put them together to make a sandwich that is as appropriate at a party as it is for a brown bag lunch.

Makes about 3 dozen
    sandwiches (6 dozen
    cookies)
Baking pan: greased cookie
    sheet
Preheat oven to 350°

½ cup butter
¼ cup sugar
¼ cup brown sugar
1 egg
¼ cup molasses
3 tablespoons honey
3 cups flour
½ teaspoon baking soda
¼ teaspoon salt
1 teaspoon ginger
½ teaspoon cinnamon
¼ teaspoon ground cloves

Orange Filling

1. Cream the butter, sugar and brown sugar.
2. Add egg, molasses and honey and blend well.
3. Stir together the flour, baking soda, salt and spices. Add gradually to the creamed mixture and blend well. Divide the dough in half, wrap each half snugly in plastic and refrigerate for 2 hours or until firm enough to roll out.
4. Dust the work surface and rolling pin generously with flour. Roll out half the dough at a time to ⅛-inch thick. Cut with a round cookie cutter about 2 inches in diameter. Lift away the excess dough and save it for re-rolling. Transfer the rounds to the cookie sheet, leaving 1 inch between them.
5. Bake for 8–10 minutes. Transfer the cookies to wire racks to cool.
6. Brush the crumbs off the wrong sides of the cookies. Spread Orange Filling generously on the wrong sides of half the cookies and cover with the remaining cookies.

Orange Filling

Makes about 1 cup

1 egg yolk
3 tablespoons orange juice
2 tablespoons grated orange
    rind
2 cups confectioners' sugar

Stir all the ingredients together and beat to a smooth consistency.

Big Fig Sandwiches

Look out—just one of these hearty sandwiches is a whole lot of cookie. They are rather homely, I'm afraid, but very friendly and delicious, a wonderful combination of oatmeal and coconut in the dough, plus a thick fig filling.

Makes about 1½ dozen sandwiches (3 dozen cookies)
Baking pan: greased cookie sheet
Preheat oven to 350°

¾ cup margarine
½ cup sugar
½ cup brown sugar
1 egg
¼ cup water
1 teaspoon vanilla
1 cup flour
2½ cups oatmeal (not the quick-cooking kind)
½ cup sweetened flaked or shredded coconut
½ teaspoon baking soda
½ teaspoon salt

Fig Filling

1. Cream the margarine, sugar and brown sugar.
2. Add the egg, water and vanilla and blend well.
3. Stir together the flour, oatmeal, coconut, baking soda and salt. Add the flour mixture to the creamed mixture and blend well.
4. Drop the dough by rounded tablespoons onto the cookie sheet, leaving 2 inches between drops. Flatten each drop with a fork dipped in flour.
5. Bake for 15 minutes. Let the cookies cool slightly on the cookie sheet and then transfer to wire racks to finish cooling.
6. Brush the crumbs off the wrong sides of the cookies. Spread Fig Filling on the wrong sides of half the cookies and cover with the remaining cookies.

Fig Filling

Makes about 1⅓ cups

1 cup finely chopped dried figs
¼ cup chopped raisins
6 tablespoons sugar
1 tablespoon butter
5 tablespoons water
2 teaspoons lemon juice
pinch of salt

Combine all the ingredients in a heavy saucepan over low heat. Bring to a boil and simmer until thick, stirring constantly, about 5–7 minutes.

Date, Nut and Cream Cheese Sandwiches

When I was a little girl, my favorite sandwich was cream cheese on date nut bread. This cookie version is a second cousin once removed, but it's still in the family. The cookies are thick and crisp, studded with bits of date and walnut and filled generously with sweet cream cheese frosting. For very pretty edges, cut the squares of rolled dough with a fluted pastry wheel.

**Makes about 28 sandwiches
(56 cookies)**
**Baking pan: greased cookie
sheet**
Preheat oven to 350°

½ cup plus 1 tablespoon
   butter or margarine
½ cup sugar
½ cup light brown sugar
1 egg
¼ cup milk
2 tablespoons dry sherry
3 cups flour
1½ teaspoons baking powder
¼ teaspoon salt
1 cup pitted dates, finely
   chopped
¾ cup chopped walnuts

**Cream Cheese Frosting (page
   122)**

1. Cream the butter, sugar and light brown sugar.

2. Add the egg, milk and sherry and blend well.

3. Stir together the flour, baking powder, salt, dates and nuts. Add to the creamed mixture and blend well. Divide the dough in half, wrap each half snugly in plastic and refrigerate for 45 minutes or until firm enough to roll out.

4. Dust the work surface and rolling pin with flour. Roll out half the dough at a time to a little less than ¼-inch thick. Cut the dough into 2-inch squares. Transfer the squares to the cookie sheet, leaving about ¾ inch between them. Gather up the excess dough for re-rolling to make more squares.

5. Bake for 12–14 minutes or until very lightly browned. Remove the hot cookies from the cookie sheet and place on wire racks to cool.

6. Brush the crumbs away from the wrong sides of the cookies. Spread Cream Cheese Frosting generously on the wrong sides of half the cookies and cover with the remaining cookies.

Cream Cheese Frosting

Makes about ¾ cup

1 tablespoon butter, room
   temperature
1 3-ounce package of cream
   cheese, room temperature
1 teaspoon vanilla
¾ cup superfine sugar, sifted
¼ cup confectioners' sugar,
   sifted
½ pinch of salt
¼ teaspoon grated orange rind
   (optional)

Cream the butter and cream cheese. Add the vanilla and blend well. Gradually add the superfine sugar and beat until smooth. Add the confectioners' sugar and salt and beat again. Stir in the grated orange rind if desired.

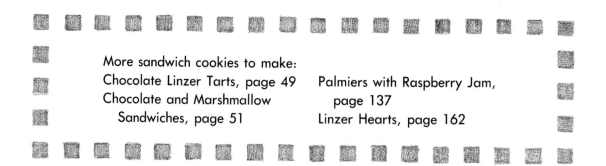

More sandwich cookies to make:
Chocolate Linzer Tarts, page 49
Chocolate and Marshmallow
   Sandwiches, page 51
Palmiers with Raspberry Jam,
   page 137
Linzer Hearts, page 162

10. Cookies to Eat on Your Coffee Break: SNACK COOKIES

Spicy Apple Cookies
Pumpkin Carrot Cookies
Chewy Fruit Squares
Iced Molasses Cookies
Orange Oatmeal Cookies
Granola Bars

Buttermilk Tea Cakes
Almond Cookies with Prune Topping
Cream Cheese and Walnut Cookies
Date Things
Golden Raisin Cookies

Of course you can snack on any cookie in this book, but in this chapter I've given you some delicious cookies that are generally a little less sweet than the others. Cookies that have a little something extra like cream cheese, granola, apple or prune butter or dried fruit. Cookies that are mild and light and won't weigh you down for the rest of the day.

Here's what you can do with snack cookies:

• Take them with you in your brown bag or lunch box.

• Serve them after school.

• Curl up in the porch swing and munch a few while you sip iced tea.

• Have a couple while you give yourself a break from typing or painting or settling a thorny legal problem.

• Eat one while you have a cup of coffee and chat with your best friend.

• Grab a handful and relax with a magazine while the baby naps.

It's the time you take—time out—as much as the cookies themselves that revitalizes you and lifts your spirits. But the cookies help.

Spicy Apple Cookies

For this easy recipe use natural apple butter and natural, unsweetened applesauce to get the best results—a soft and spicy cookie with a mellow apple flavor. The recipe makes lots of cookies, so you won't have to worry about restocking the cookie jar for a while.

Makes about 6½ dozen cookies
Baking pan: greased cookie sheet
Preheat oven to 375°

½ cup butter
½ cup sugar
½ cup dark brown sugar
1 egg
½ cup unsweetened applesauce
½ cup natural apple butter (with nothing added)
2 cups flour
1 teaspoon baking soda
½ teaspoon salt
½ teaspoon cinnamon
½ teaspoon nutmeg
¼ teaspoon ground cloves
1 cup raisins

1. Cream the butter, sugar and dark brown sugar.

2. Add the egg and blend well.

3. Add the applesauce and apple butter and blend well.

4. Stir together the flour, baking soda, salt and spices. Stir in the raisins. Add to the creamed mixture and blend well.

5. Drop the dough by teaspoons onto the cookie sheet, leaving 1½ inches between drops.

6. Bake for 10 minutes. Let the cookies cool slightly on the cookie sheet and then remove to wire racks to finish cooling.

Pumpkin Carrot Cookies

Here's a simple drop cookie with a good, hearty taste of carrots, pumpkin and nuts. It's cakelike and not too sweet; if you prefer a sweeter cookie, flatten the drops before baking and top them with Cream Cheese Frosting when they are cool.

Makes about 3–3½ dozen
  cookies
Baking pan: greased cookie
  sheet
Preheat oven to 350°

½ cup butter
1 cup margarine
½ cup sugar
½ cup brown sugar
1 cup canned pumpkin
½ cup finely grated carrot
1 egg
1 teaspoon vanilla
2 cups flour
1 teaspoon baking powder
½ teaspoon baking soda
½ teaspoon salt
1 teaspoon cinnamon
½ teaspoon nutmeg
½ cup chopped walnuts or
  pecans

1. Cream the butter, margarine, sugar and brown sugar.

2. Add the pumpkin, carrot, egg and vanilla and blend well.

3. Stir together the flour, baking powder, baking soda, salt, spices and nuts. Add to the creamed mixture and blend well.

4. Drop the dough by rounded teaspoons onto the cookie sheet, leaving 1 inch between drops.

5. Bake for 12–15 minutes. Let the cookies cool on the cookie sheet for a minute or two and then transfer to wire racks to finish cooling.

Variation

Flatten each drop of dough either with a fork dipped in flour or with the flour-dusted bottom of a glass. When the cookies are baked and cool, spread with Cream Cheese Frosting (page 122) and top with a few slivers of candied ginger.

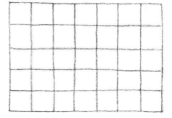

Chewy Fruit Squares

The squares are spicy and moist, a little like fruit cake. Use a variety of dried fruit and you'll find that every bite is a flavor surprise. If the fruit seems overly dry and tough, chop it up and let it sit in a little water, stirring occasionally, until softened. Dry on paper towels before adding to the dough.

Makes 35 squares
Baking pan: 13″ × 9″, greased
Preheat oven to 375°

½ cup butter
½ cup sugar
½ cup brown sugar
1 egg
¼ cup orange juice
1 teaspoon vanilla
2¼ cups flour
1 teaspoon baking powder
½ teaspoon baking soda
½ teaspoon salt
1 teaspoon cinnamon
½ cup raisins
1 cup chopped dried fruit:
    apricots, peaches, prunes,
    apples, pears or any
    combination of these
¾ cup chopped nuts

1. Cream the butter, sugar and brown sugar.

2. Add the egg, orange juice and vanilla and blend well.

3. Stir together the flour, baking powder, baking soda, salt and cinnamon. Add the raisins, chopped fruit and nuts and stir well to coat all the sticky bits of fruit. Add to the creamed mixture and blend well.

4. Spread the dough evenly in the pan.

5. Bake for 20 minutes. The edges will be brown and a knife inserted in the center will come out clean. Do not overbake or the bottom will burn. Place the pan on a wire rack and allow the dough to cool. Cut in squares and remove the squares carefully.

Iced Molasses Cookies

Each cookie is like a little iced cake—moist and tender with a mild molasses and lovely orange (or lemon) flavor. The dough is very soft and spreads a great deal during baking.

Makes about 2½–3 dozen
   cookies
Baking pan: greased cookie
   sheet
Preheat oven to 350°

5 tablespoons butter
¼ cup sugar
¼ cup brown sugar
½ cup molasses
1 egg
1 teaspoon vanilla
¼ cup water
2 cups flour
2 teaspoons baking soda
¼ teaspoon salt
2 teaspoons grated orange or
   lemon rind

Milk Glaze (page 165; double
   the recipe if you want to ice
   all the cookies)

1. Melt the butter, sugar, brown sugar and molasses in a heavy saucepan over low heat, stirring constantly until the sugar and brown sugar are dissolved. Remove from the heat and allow to cool.

2. Add the egg, vanilla and water to the sugar mixture and blend well.

3. Stir together the flour, baking soda, salt and grated rind. Add to the sugar mixture and blend well.

4. Drop the dough by rounded teaspoons onto the cookie sheet, leaving 2 inches between drops.

5. Bake for 10 minutes. Let the cookies cool on the cookie sheet for a minute or two and then transfer to wire racks to finish cooling.

6. When the cookies are cool, spread with Milk Glaze.

Orange Oatmeal Cookies

Another of my top ten favorites. I like to keep a few in the freezer and take them out to thaw one at a time so I don't eat too many at a single sitting. It's simply a great oatmeal cookie, rich and buttery, with a light orange flavor.

Makes about 2½ dozen cookies
Baking pan: greased cookie sheet
Preheat oven to 350°

¾ cup butter
½ cup sugar
½ cup brown sugar
1 egg
¼ cup frozen orange juice concentrate
1 teaspoon vanilla
1 cup flour
3 cups oatmeal (not the quick-cooking kind)
¾ teaspoon salt
½ cup chopped walnuts or pecans

1. Cream the butter, sugar and brown sugar.

2. Add the egg, orange juice concentrate and vanilla and blend well.

3. Stir together the flour, oatmeal, salt and chopped nuts. Add to the creamed mixture and blend well.

4. Drop the dough by rounded teaspoons onto the cookie sheet, leaving 2 inches between drops. Flatten each drop slightly with a fork dipped in flour.

5. Bake for 12 minutes. Allow the cookies to cool on the cookie sheet for a minute or two and then carefully transfer to wire racks to finish cooling.

Granola Bars

This recipe, made with granola and nuts, is extremely easy to do and yields a bar that tastes something like a sweet biscuit, mild with a pleasant crumb. It is important to use the correct size pan for these—and all other—bars. You may find the stiff batter is difficult to spread all the way to the edges of the pan. Just get as close as possible; the dough will spread further during baking.

Makes 32 bars
Baking pan: 15½" × 10½",
 greased and floured
Preheat oven to 400°

1 cup margarine
1 cup brown sugar
2 eggs
1 teaspoon vanilla
2 cups flour
2 cups plain granola
1 teaspoon baking soda
½ teaspoon salt
¾ cup chopped walnuts or
 pecans

1. Cream the margarine and brown sugar.
2. Add the eggs and vanilla and blend well.
3. Stir together the flour, granola, baking soda, salt and chopped nuts. Add to the creamed mixture and blend well.
4. Spread the dough evenly in the pan.
5. Bake for 10 minutes. Place the pan on a wire rack and let the dough cool. Cut in squares and remove the squares carefully.

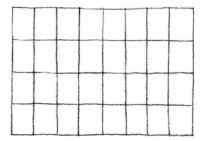

Buttermilk Tea Cakes

A great favorite of mine, especially for a late afternoon pick-me-up with, of course, a cup of tea. It's a comforting, soothing cookie, simple and delicate with crisp edges and a crumbly center. The dough is very sticky to work with, so use a generous amount of flour during the initial rolling. It gets easier to roll as the extra flour is incorporated into the dough.

Makes about 2 dozen cookies
Baking pan: greased cookie
   sheet
Preheat oven to 350°

½ cup butter
¾ cup sugar
1 egg
1 teaspoon vanilla
1 teaspoon baking soda
¼ cup buttermilk
2 cups flour
¼ teaspoon salt

1. Cream the butter and sugar.
2. Add the egg and vanilla and blend well.
3. Dissolve the baking soda in the buttermilk. Add to the creamed mixture and blend well.
4. Stir together the flour and salt. Add to the creamed mixture and blend well.
5. Dust the work surface and rolling pin very generously with flour. Roll out the dough to ¼-inch thick and cut with a biscuit or cookie cutter 1½–2 inches in diameter. Transfer the cakes to the cookie sheet. Gather up the excess dough and save it for re-rolling.
6. Bake for 10–12 minutes, until golden. Transfer the cakes to wire racks to cool.

Almond Cookies with Prune Topping

Refrigerator cookies like this one, sliced from a log of dough, are a tremendous convenience: Just cut as many as you need at one time and store the remainder of the log in the refrigerator for another occasion. This crisp, crunchy almond cookie is topped with prune butter, a wonderful combination.

Makes about 2½ dozen cookies
Baking pan: greased cookie
   sheet
Preheat oven to 375°

½ cup butter
½ cup sugar
¼ cup brown sugar
1 egg
1 teaspoon vanilla
½ teaspoon almond extract
1¾ cups flour
½ teaspoon baking powder
¼ teaspoon salt
½ cup ground almonds
1 cup prune butter
whole almonds

1. Cream the butter, sugar and brown sugar.
2. Add the egg, vanilla and almond extract and blend well.
3. Stir together the flour, baking powder, salt and ground almonds. Add to the creamed mixture and blend well. Refrigerate the dough until firm.
4. Shape the dough into a log about 2 inches in diameter. Wrap snugly in plastic and refrigerate again until firm.
5. Unwrap the log and cut in slices ¼-inch thick. If you like, cut only as many slices as you need right now and refrigerate or freeze the remainder of the log. Place the slices on the cookie sheet, leaving 1½ inches between them.
6. Bake for 12 minutes. Let the cookies cool slightly on the cookie sheet and then transfer to wire racks to finish cooling.
7. Spread a small dollop of prune butter on each cookie and top with a whole almond.

Cream Cheese and Walnut Cookies

Rich little morsels like these—sweet cream cheese dough rolled in chopped walnuts—will disappear as fast as you can make them. Try a variation, using currants, pecans or dates. Better still, make some of each.

Makes about 2½ dozen cookies
Baking pan: greased and
    floured cookie sheet
Preheat oven to 350°

½ cup butter
1 3-ounce package of cream
    cheese, softened
½ cup sugar
1 egg
1 teaspoon vanilla
1½ cups flour
1 teaspoon baking powder
¼ teaspoon salt
1 cup finely chopped walnuts

1. Cream the butter and cream cheese.
2. Add the sugar and cream again.
3. Add the egg and vanilla and blend well.
4. Stir together the flour, baking powder and salt. Add to the creamed mixture and blend well. Refrigerate the dough for 1 hour or until firm.
5. Break off small pieces of dough and shape into balls about 1 inch in diameter. Press one side of each ball into the chopped walnuts. Place the balls, walnut side up, on the cookie sheet, leaving 2 inches between them. Flatten each ball slightly.

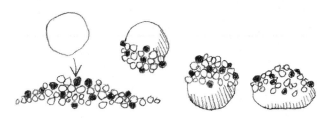

6. Bake for 12 minutes. Let the cookies cool for a minute or two on the cookie sheet and then transfer to wire racks to finish cooling.

Variations

1. Stir ½ cup currants into the flour mixture before adding it to the creamed mixture.
2. Instead of dunking each ball of dough in chopped walnuts, flatten each ball and top with a whole pecan or half a date. Be sure to press the nut or date firmly into the dough.

Date Things

Kathy Sizemore gave me this oddly named recipe; I can just imagine one of her kids saying, "Hey, Mom, please make some of those cookies, you know, those date things." Whatever you decide to call them, they will still be scrumptious little cookies wrapped around date halves that get soft and mellow during baking.

Makes about 3 dozen cookies
Baking pan: greased cookie
   sheet
Preheat oven to 350°

1 cup butter
½ cup brown sugar
2 egg yolks
1 teaspoon vanilla
2¼ cups flour
½ teaspoon salt
¼ teaspoon cinnamon
pitted dates, cut in half
2 egg whites mixed with 1
   teaspoon water
1½ cups finely chopped
   walnuts or pecans

1. Cream the butter and brown sugar.
2. Add the egg yolks and vanilla and blend well.
3. Stir together the flour, salt and cinnamon. Add to the creamed mixture and blend well.
4. Take a piece of dough a little smaller than a walnut and push half a date into it. Press the dough around the date to cover it, pinching the dough together. Repeat until the dough is used up.

5. Dip each cookie in egg white and then roll it in chopped nuts.
6. Bake for 12 minutes. Transfer the cookies to wire racks to cool.

Golden Raisin Cookies

These cookies have a taste and texture a little like tea cakes or tea bread—light with a soft crumb and not too sweet (except when you bite into a raisin). The cream cheese in the dough makes the cookies extra-good.

Makes about 2½ dozen cookies
Baking pan: greased cookie
   sheet
Preheat oven to 375°

5 tablespoons butter
1 3-ounce package of cream
   cheese, softened
¾ cup sugar
1 egg
1 teaspoon vanilla
2 teaspoons lemon juice
2 cups flour
½ teaspoon baking soda
½ teaspoon salt
1 cup golden raisins

1. Cream the butter and cream cheese.
2. Add the sugar and cream again.
3. Add the egg, vanilla and lemon juice and blend well.
4. Stir together the flour, baking soda and salt. Add to the creamed mixture and blend well.
5. Add the raisins and mix thoroughly.
6. Drop the dough by rounded teaspoons onto the cookie sheet, leaving 1 inch between drops. Using a glass with a flat bottom, dipped in flour, flatten each drop of dough to about ¼-inch thick.
7. Bake for 15 minutes. Allow the cookies to cool on the cookie sheet for a minute or two and then transfer to wire racks to finish cooling.

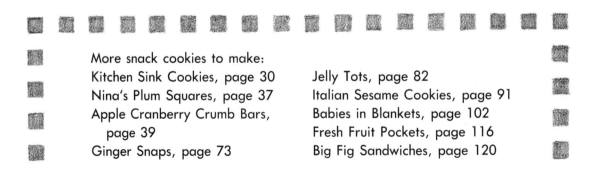

11. How to Impress Your Friends and Relations: PARTY COOKIES

Rolled Marzipan Cookies
Palmiers with Raspberry Jam
Spiced Sherry Cookies
Chocolate Almond Leaves
Meringue Surprises
Rich Walnut Bites

Pastel Pinwheels
Fancy Lace Wafers
Chestnut Butter Cups
Brown Edge Wafers
Annie's Ladyfingers

Parties call for special foods and nothing fills the bill better than fancy cookies. You may opt for simple elegance and serve Brown Edge Wafers or Annie's Ladyfingers, or you may want to dazzle your guests with Palmiers with Raspberry Jam or Chestnut Butter Cups. Whatever recipe you choose from this chapter, the company will be suitably impressed with the beauty and delectability of your cookies.

Presentation is very important in creating a party atmosphere. If you have storage room, prepare several small plates of cookies instead of one large platter; as the cookies are eaten and the plate begins to look skimpy, remove it and replace it with a fresh, full plate.

The prettiest cookies look best set out in one layer on a plate or small serving platter that is covered first with a lacy paper doily. Cookies of simple shapes will look wonderful in graduated layers, but don't stack them too high. If you have a tiered dish, arrange one kind of cookie on each level. And don't forget the candlelight and flowers.

Rolled Marzipan Cookies

This unusual cookie is wonderfully chewy, with a distinctive orange flavor and the richness of ground almonds. Each cookie starts life—before baking—as a flat round with a little decoration in the middle. During baking it puffs up and spreads out and comes from the oven with a crisp, cracked surface. Delicious with sherbet topped with fruit sauce. Note that the recipe contains no flour.

Makes about 25 cookies
Baking pan: greased cookie sheet
Preheat oven to 375°

4 egg yolks
¼ teaspoon almond extract
1 cup sugar
1½ cups ground almonds
1 tablespoon grated orange rind
confectioners' sugar
1 egg white

1. Stir together the egg yolks and almond extract.

2. Stir together the sugar, ground almonds and orange rind. Add to the egg yolks and blend well, first with a spoon and then with your hands to make a smooth paste. Divide the dough in half, wrap each half snugly in plastic and refrigerate for half an hour or until firm enough to roll out.

3. Dust the work surface and rolling pin with confectioners' sugar. Roll out half the dough at a time to ⅛-inch thick. For each cookie, cut out a scalloped or plain round about 2 inches in diameter, plus a little extra piece to decorate the top. You may cut the extra piece with a knife, aspic cutter or canapé cutter. Dab a bit of egg white in the middle of each round and press the extra piece in place. Transfer the cookies to the cookie sheet, leaving ¾ inch between rounds. Gather up the excess dough for re-rolling to make more rounds.

4. Bake for 8–10 minutes. Allow the cookies to cool on the cookie sheet for 2 to 3 minutes and then transfer to wire racks to finish cooling.

Palmiers with Raspberry Jam

Palmiers (a French word pronounced *pahl*-mee-yay) are cookies made from an amazing dough called puff pastry. When baked, these cookies puff up into many flaky, crunchy layers of delicately sweet, buttery dough. Eat them one at a time in the traditional way or sandwiched with raspberry jam, as I like them.

Puff pastry is often said to be extremely difficult to make. This reputation is undeserved. The process is time-consuming and somewhat laborious because there are many steps to complete, but puff pastry is not hard to make if you follow the instructions and drawings attentively. Do it for the challenge and the pleasure of working with such a magical dough—and if you've ever sampled a really topnotch palmier, you'll want to do it for the great taste.

Makes about 2 dozen
    sandwiches (4 dozen
    cookies)
Baking pan: greased cookie
    sheet
Preheat oven to 400°

2 cups flour
pinch of salt
1 cup unsalted butter, cold but
    not frozen
½ cup ice water
sugar
raspberry jam

1. Stir together the flour and salt. Cut in 4 tablespoons of the butter (this may be done in a food processor). The mixture should be like fine crumbs.

2. Work in as much of the ½ cup of ice water as you need to make a ball of dough that is not sticky and holds together firmly. Refrigerate the dough for 15 minutes.

3. Meanwhile, cut up the remaining butter and, on a piece of waxed paper, arrange the pieces to make a slab ¾-inch thick and as square as you can get it. Set aside until the ball of dough comes out of the refrigerator.

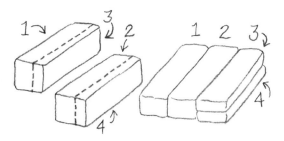

4. On a floured work surface, roll out the dough to a rectangle about ¼-inch thick. Put the square of butter in the center and fold the dough around the butter as shown in the drawing.

Turn the dough package over onto a plate or pan, seam side down, and refrigerate for 15 minutes.

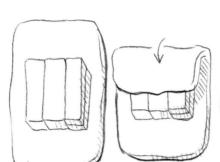

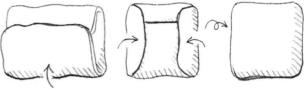

5. Place the dough, seam side down, on a well-floured work surface and roll it out to a rectangle about ¼-inch thick. Fold the dough in thirds as shown and turn it 90°, from horizontal to vertical.

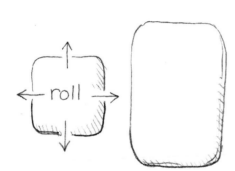

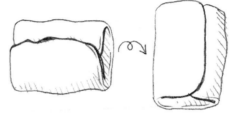

Roll the dough out again, to a rectangle ¼-inch thick. Fold in thirds and place the dough, flap side down, on the plate or pan. Refrigerate for 15 minutes.

6. Repeat step 5 two more times.

7. Sprinkle sugar generously on the work surface. Roll out the dough to a square ⅛-inch thick. It is crucial to sprinkle more sugar *under* the dough whenever the dough sticks to the work surface and *over* the dough when the rolling pin sticks to the dough. Be sure to check underneath the dough often because the dough gets quite sticky. The dough is very stretchy, so it will take a lot of rolling to make the square.

8. When you have finally achieved a square, mark it lightly in sixths as shown in the drawing.

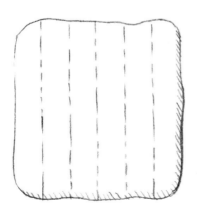

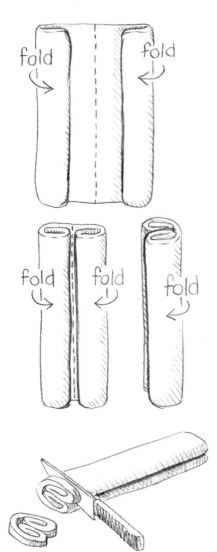

Then sprinkle the dough with sugar and fold up as shown.

9. Transfer the long roll to an ungreased cookie sheet, placing it on the diagonal if necessary. Cover with plastic wrap and place in the freezer for 30 minutes.

10. When the dough comes out of the freezer you may work with the entire roll if you like, but I prefer to cut it in half, return one half (wrapped snugly in plastic) to the refrigerator and work with the remaining half.

Put the folded dough on a cutting board and use a very sharp knife to cut slices about ⅛–¼-inch thick. An ordinary palmier is about ¼-inch thick; I prefer to cut these a bit thinner since they will be sandwiched together in pairs with the jam.

Cut about 4 slices at a time. Sprinkle one side of each slice with sugar and place it sugar-side down on a greased cookie sheet. Leave 2 inches between slices because they spread tremendously during baking. (They do shrink somewhat toward the end of the baking period.) Continue cutting slices and sugaring them until the cookie sheet is filled. Sprinkle sugar on the tops of the slices.

By now the dough is getting soft, so return it to the freezer to firm up.

11. Bake the slices for 7 minutes on the middle shelf of the oven. (Do not try to bake two cookie sheets at once unless your oven can accommodate two sheets side by side.)

After 7 minutes the cookies will still be pale. Don't worry about this. Turn the cookies over and bake for 7 more minutes.

The cookies should be golden brown after the total 14 minutes of baking. If they are not, you may bake them for another minute or two on each side. Watch them very, very carefully.

Take the cookies out of the oven and transfer them to wire racks at once. When they are cool, spread jam on half the cookies and cover with the other half.

Spiced Sherry Cookies

Used as flavoring for cookie dough, wine or spirits rarely overpower the baked cookie itself and often make it quite intriguing. This small cookie, tasting subtly of sweet sherry, is light and spicy with a tart lemon glaze to enhance it.

Makes about 7½ dozen cookies

Baking pan: greased cookie sheet

Preheat oven to 350°

½ cup butter
1 cup light brown sugar
1 egg
5 tablespoons sweet sherry
2–2¼ cups flour
1 teaspoon baking soda
1 teaspoon cinnamon
½ teaspoon ginger
¼ teaspoon ground cloves
¼ teaspoon salt
½ cup ground almonds

Lemon Glaze (page 166)

1. Cream the butter and light brown sugar.
2. Add the egg and sherry and blend well.
3. Stir together 2 cups of the flour, the baking soda, spices, salt and ground almonds. Add to the creamed mixture and blend well. You may have to add up to another ¼ cup of flour to make a dough that holds together and is not too sticky. Divide the dough in half, wrap each half snugly in plastic and refrigerate until firm enough to roll out.
4. Dust the work surface and rolling pin with flour. Roll out half the dough at a time to a little less than ¼-inch thick. Cut with a round or scalloped cookie cutter about 1½ inches in diameter. With a spatula, transfer the rounds to the cookie sheet, leaving 1 inch between them. Gather up the excess dough for re-rolling to make more rounds.
5. Bake for 6 minutes. Allow the cookies to cool on the cookie sheet for a minute and then transfer to wire racks to finish cooling.
6. When the cookies are cool, spread each one with a thin layer of Lemon Glaze.

 Chocolate Almond Leaves

I happen to love this oak leaf shape—and the cookie tastes pretty good, too! It's crisp and almond-flavored, not too sweet, with a hint of lemon. The chocolate coating (one side only) gives it a wonderful semi-sweet bite. Leave it plain or decorate it with slivered almonds as shown in the drawing.

Makes about 2½ dozen cookies
Baking pan: greased and
   floured cookie sheet
Preheat oven to 375°

¾ cup almond paste
2 egg yolks
¾ cup butter
6 tablespoons sugar
1 teaspoon vanilla
1 tablespoon grated lemon rind
2 tablespoons lemon juice
1½–1¾ cups flour
½ teaspoon salt
7 squares (7 ounces) semi-
   sweet chocolate, melted
slivered almonds (optional)

1. Mash the almond paste with the egg yolks until soft and well blended.

2. Add the butter, bit by bit, mixing until well blended.

3. Add the sugar and blend well.

4. Add the vanilla, grated lemon rind and lemon juice and blend well.

5. Stir together 1½ cups of the flour and the salt and add gradually to the almond paste mixture. If the dough seems very sticky, add the extra ¼ cup of flour. Divide the dough in half, wrap each half snugly in plastic and refrigerate for 1½ hours or until firm enough to roll out.

6. Dust the work surface and rolling pin generously with flour. Roll half the dough at a time to ⅛-inch thick. Cut with a leaf-shaped cookie cutter and use a spatula to transfer the leaves to the cookie sheet, leaving 1 inch between them. Gather up the excess dough and save it for re-rolling.

7. Bake for 10 minutes or until golden. Let the cookies cool slightly on the cookie sheet and then transfer to wire racks to finish cooling.

8. When the cookies are cool, spread or brush the back of each leaf with melted chocolate. Decorate with slivered almonds, if you like, while the chocolate is soft. Allow the chocolate to harden. Serve the cookies chocolate side up.

Meringue Surprises

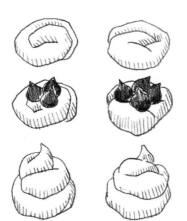

The surprise is the chocolate chips tucked in the center of each meringue. When a dear friend of mine had to exclude wheat flour from his diet, I made these confections for him to nibble so he wouldn't feel deprived of the sweet pastries to which he was addicted. Now he can eat regular baked goods again, but he still enjoys these meringues.

Makes about 3 dozen cookies
Baking pan: 2 greased and
    floured cookie sheets
Preheat oven to 250°

4 egg whites, room
    temperature
pinch of cream of tartar
pinch of salt
1 teaspoon vanilla
1 cup sugar
chocolate chips

1. Stir the egg whites, cream of tartar, salt and vanilla in a deep bowl. Beat until the egg whites hold soft peaks.

2. Add the sugar, 1 tablespoon at a time, while continuing to beat the egg whites. Beat until the mixture holds stiff peaks. All the sugar must be dissolved.

3. Fit a pastry bag with a #10 (large round) tip or cut a tiny bit off the corner of a sturdy plastic bag.

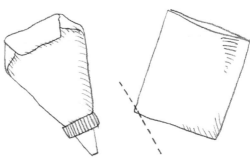

Spoon the meringue into the bag and pipe rounds about 1½ inches in diameter onto the cookie sheets, leaving about 1 inch between rounds. Try to fit at least 18 rounds on each cookie sheet because you will have to discard any leftover meringue. Place 3 or 4 chocolate chips in the center of each round. Now pipe a cap to cover each little mound of chocolate chips. Follow the drawing for guidance.

4. Meringues are not actually baked to hardness; they are baked briefly and then allowed to dry for several hours in a warm but unlit oven.

Put the cookie sheets in the oven for 30 minutes. Then turn off the heat and leave the cookie sheets in the oven for at least 4–5 hours (or preferably overnight) without opening the oven door.

Use a spatula to remove the meringues carefully from the cookie sheets.

 Rich Walnut Bites

Blanche Small, my grandmother, has been making these cookies as long as I can remember. At 85, she still bakes raisin bread and chocolate cake and lots of cookies, even though she knows she shouldn't eat them herself. Somehow she manages to find eager takers for all of it, which pleases her because then she can bake more.

Makes about 8 dozen cookies
Baking pan: ungreased cookie
   sheet
Preheat oven to 350°

2 cups salted butter, softened
1¼ cups confectioners' sugar
2 teaspoons vanilla
3½ cups flour
2 cups chopped walnuts
confectioners' sugar (optional)

1. Cream the butter and 1¼ cups confectioners' sugar.
2. Add the vanilla and blend well.
3. Add the flour and blend well.
4. Add the chopped walnuts and blend well.
5. Break off small pieces of dough and shape them into walnut-size balls. Place them on the cookie sheet, leaving about ½ inch between balls.
6. Bake for 15 minutes. Let the cookies cool slightly on the cookie sheet and then remove from the cookie sheet to wire racks to finish cooling. If you like, you may coat the warm cookies in confectioners' sugar: Put some confectioners' sugar in a plastic bag, add a few cookies at a time and shake the bag gently. Repeat until all the cookies are coated.

Pastel Pinwheels

Pinwheels are great fun to make. In this case, the buttery dough is rolled, chilled, sliced and baked to make pretty spirals of pink and green. You may, of course, prefer other colors: try pink and white (uncolored dough), green and white, yellow and green or yellow and pink.

Makes about 3 dozen cookies
Baking pan: greased cookie sheet
Preheat oven to 350°

¾ cup butter or margarine
1 cup sugar
1 egg
1 teaspoon vanilla
2¼ cups flour
½ teaspoon baking powder
¼ teaspoon salt
red and green food coloring

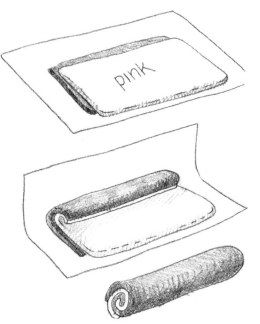

1. Cream the butter and sugar.
2. Add the egg and vanilla and blend well.
3. Stir together the flour, baking powder and salt. Add to the creamed mixture and blend well.
4. Divide the dough in half. Color one half pink by working in a few drops of red food coloring. Color the other half light green with a few drops of green food coloring. Be sure to blend each color well. Refrigerate the dough for several hours or until firm enough to roll out.
5. Roll out the pink dough on a piece of well-floured waxed paper, making a rectangle about 6 × 12 inches and about ¼-inch thick. Slide the waxed paper and dough onto the back of a cookie sheet and refrigerate until firm. Repeat this process with the green dough.
6. Remove the dough from the refrigerator. Turn the pink dough over (waxed paper up) and place over the green dough, about ½ inch from the long edge. Peel the waxed paper away from the pink dough.

Roll up the two colors of dough from long side to long side, using the remaining waxed paper to help. Try to roll the two doughs together tightly. Wrap snugly in the waxed paper and freeze the dough for 1 hour.
7. Unwrap the dough and use a sharp, serrated knife to cut slices ⅛-inch thick. (If the dough softens, return it to the freezer for 15 minutes.) Place on the cookie sheet, leaving 1½ inches between slices.
8. Bake for 10–12 minutes. Let the cookies cool slightly on the cookie sheet and then transfer to wire racks to finish cooling.

Fancy Lace Wafers

I love this cookie because it is like my favorite butter crunch candy. The batter is indeed buttery, sweet and crunchy with almonds, and the baked wafers are dipped in melted chocolate and then in more chopped almonds. Annie Wright, chef, caterer and also recipe-tester for this book, says "yum, yum, yum" about these cookies and she should know.

Makes about 5½ dozen cookies
Baking pan: greased and
   floured cookie sheet
Preheat oven to 350°

1 cup finely chopped almonds
½ cup butter
½ cup sugar
1 tablespoon flour
2 tablespoons milk
6 or more semi-sweet chocolate
   squares, melted

1. Put ½ cup of the chopped almonds plus the butter, sugar, flour and milk in a heavy saucepan. Cook, stirring constantly, over low heat until the butter is melted.

2. Drop the batter by scant teaspoons onto the cookie sheet, leaving 3 inches between drops. The batter will spread tremendously during baking.

3. Bake for 5–7 minutes, until golden and bubbling. Let the cookies cool on the cookie sheet *for only a minute or two.* Use a spatula to loosen all the cookies at one time. Transfer the cookies to wire racks. If the cookies cool too much, you will not be able to detach them cleanly from the cookie sheet; in that case, return them to the oven to warm up and then continue removing them with the spatula.

4. Very gently dip half of the top side of each cookie first into a small bowl of melted chocolate and then into a small bowl of the remaining chopped almonds. Place on wire racks while the chocolate hardens.

Chestnut Butter Cups

I don't get to indulge in chestnuts nearly often enough. Perhaps that's why these little dough cups with sweet, thick Chestnut Butter filling and grated chocolate topping seem so special and festive to me. Perfect for an autumn or winter party.

Note: A gem muffin pan is simply a miniature muffin pan, with cups measuring almost 2 inches across the top.

Makes about 4 dozen cups
Baking pan: gem muffin pan,
    ungreased
Preheat oven to 350°

1 cup butter, softened
2 3-ounce packages of cream
    cheese, softened
2 cups flour

Chestnut Butter
grated semi-sweet chocolate

1. Cream the butter and cream cheese.
2. Add the flour and blend well. Divide the dough into four equal parts, wrap each part snugly in plastic and refrigerate for 2 hours or until firm.
3. Make Chestnut Butter while the dough is chilling and keep it refrigerated until half an hour before you want to fill the baked cups.
4. Take one package of dough at a time out of the refrigerator. Divide the package of dough into 12 balls of equal size. Press a ball into each muffin cup, lining the bottom and sides evenly with dough.
5. Bake for 15–20 minutes. Let the cups cool in the pan for several minutes and then transfer carefully to wire racks to finish cooling.

Repeat steps 4 and 5 with the remaining packages of chilled dough.

6. Pack Chestnut Butter into a pastry bag fitted with a large round or star tip. Pipe a mound of Chestnut Butter into each dough cup. If the butter begins to get too soft for piping, put the pastry bag in the refrigerator for a few minutes.

Sprinkle the tops of the cups with grated chocolate. Refrigerate the finished cookies until you are almost ready to serve them.

Chestnut Butter

Makes about 2 cups

3 egg yolks
¾ cup canned chestnut purée
½ cup sugar
3 teaspoons vanilla
1½ cups butter, cold but not frozen

1. Beat the egg yolks until light and lemon-colored.
2. Add the chestnut purée and blend well.
3. Add the sugar and vanilla and blend well.
4. Add the butter in small chunks, one at a time, beating each piece in until it is completely incorporated. Refrigerate the Chestnut Butter until half an hour before it is needed. When you use it, it should be pliable but not soft.

 # Brown Edge Wafers

This is a cookie of understated elegance—thin, crisp and subtle, with a faint flavor of orange imparted by the orange liqueur.

Makes about 4 dozen cookies
Baking pan: greased cookie sheet
Preheat oven to 400°

¾ cup butter
¾ cup sugar
3 egg yolks
6 tablespoons orange liqueur
3 cups flour
¼ teaspoon salt

1. Cream the butter and sugar.
2. Add the egg yolks and orange liqueur and blend well.
3. Stir together the flour and salt and add to the creamed mixture. Blend well to make a soft dough. Divide the dough in half, wrap each half snugly in plastic and refrigerate for 1 hour or until firm enough to roll out.
4. Dust the work surface and rolling pin with flour. Roll out half the dough at a time to a little less than ¼-inch thick. Cut out rounds with a cookie cutter about 2 inches in diameter. Use a spatula to transfer the rounds to a cookie sheet, leaving ½ inch between them. Gather up the excess dough and save it for re-rolling.
5. Bake for 10–12 minutes. Let the cookies cool slightly on the cookie sheet and then remove to wire racks to finish cooling.

Annie's Ladyfingers

With great persistence, Annie Wright developed this recipe for perfect ladyfingers. They are a beautiful pale yellow and tan, crisp on the outside, tender and cakelike on the inside, with a delicate, mild flavor. Any party—especially tea, coffee and sherry parties—would be vastly improved by the presence of Annie's Ladyfingers.

Makes about 2 dozen cookies
Baking pan: greased and
floured cookie sheet
Preheat oven to 350°

3 egg yolks
¼ cup sugar
½ cup confectioners' sugar
3 egg whites
⅛ teaspoon salt
2 tablespoons sugar
1 teaspoon vanilla
¾ cup cake flour

1. In one bowl beat the egg yolks, ¼ cup sugar and ½ cup confectioners' sugar until light, about 5 minutes.

2. In another bowl beat the egg whites, salt, 2 tablespoons sugar and vanilla until stiff but not dry.

3. Fold the egg yolk mixture into the egg white mixture.

4. Fold the cake flour into the egg mixture.

5. Spoon the batter into a pastry bag fitted with a round tip, about ½ inch in diameter. (I simply use the plastic coupler with no metal tip at all.) Pipe 2½-inch strips of batter onto the cookie sheet, leaving 1 inch between strips.

6. Bake for 8–10 minutes. Let the cookies cool on the cookie sheet for a minute and then transfer to wire racks to finish cooling.

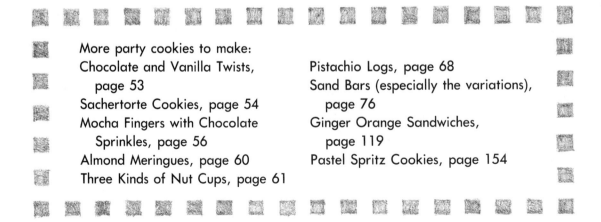

12. Halloween, Christmas, Valentine's Day and Easter: HOLIDAY COOKIES

Pumpkin Pumpkins
Christmas Rings
Gingerbread Angels
Pastel Spritz Cookies
Florentines
Chocolate Almond Pretzels

Gingerbread Wreaths
Sugar Cookie Ornaments
Cinnamon Sweethearts
Chocolate Shortbread Hearts
Linzer Hearts
Fancy Easter Eggs

What would Christmas be without Christmas cookies? It just wouldn't be the same. Everyone looks forward to these once-a-year treats, the cookies you bake only at Christmas. Along with other once-a-year events like caroling and tree-trimming, they make the Christmas festivities memorable. In this chapter you'll find some of my favorite Christmas cookies for you to add to your own family favorites—gingerbread wreaths and angels, sugar cookie ornaments, buttery Christmas rings, little pink and green spritz trees.

What Christmas cookies do for Christmas, other special cookies can do for other holidays, too. How about making a batch of pumpkin cookies for the friendly ghosts parading the streets on Halloween? Or sending ribbon-trimmed packages of heart cookies to your ten most beloved valentines. Or serving fancy Easter egg cookies with brunch on Easter morning when the egg hunters return.

So bring on the apple cider, the champagne or the wassail bowl and a big plate of fragrant, delicious holiday cookies and let's celebrate.

Pumpkin Pumpkins

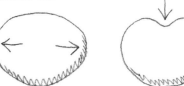

Give these Halloween cookies to all the goblins, monsters and ghosts who come knocking on your door. The cookies are soft and cakelike with a spicy, pumpkin taste, decorated with raisins, nuts, small candies and bits of dried fruit. Be sure to press the decorations very firmly into the cookie dough; the cookies puff up during baking and any loose decorations will pop right off.

Makes about 3 dozen cookies
Baking pan: greased cookie
   sheet
Preheat oven to 350°

1 cup margarine
½ cup sugar
½ cup brown sugar
1 cup canned pumpkin
1 egg
1 teaspoon vanilla
2¼ cups flour
1 teaspoon baking powder
½ teaspoon baking soda
1 teaspoon cinnamon
½ teaspoon nutmeg
¼ teaspoon allspice

For decorating:
gumdrops, candy-coated
   chocolate drops, cinnamon
   redhots, raisins, dried fruit,
   pieces of nuts

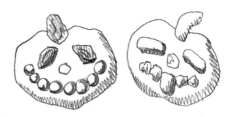

1. Cream the margarine, sugar and brown sugar.

2. Add the pumpkin and blend well.

3. Add the egg and vanilla and blend well.

4. Stir together the flour, baking powder, baking soda and spices. Add to the creamed mixture and blend well. Refrigerate the dough for ½ hour.

5. Drop the dough by tablespoons onto the cookie sheet, leaving 1½ inches between drops. Use a glass with a flat bottom, dipped in flour, to flatten each drop to a slightly elongated round, a little less than ¼-inch thick. This is the basic pumpkin shape. Push in the top edge where the stem would be.

6. Decorate each cookie with gumdrops, raisins, nuts and other tidbits to make jack-o'-lantern faces. Add half a nut or a strip of dried fruit for the stem. Be sure to press each decoration firmly into the cookie because the cookie will puff up during baking and push off any loose decorations.

7. Bake for 12–15 minutes. Let the cookies cool on the cookie sheet for a few minutes and then transfer to wire racks to finish cooling.

Christmas Rings

When I asked my mother, Claire Javna, for her favorite cookie recipe, she sent me this one. I hadn't tasted these cookies in many years, but the minute I popped one in my mouth I remembered them perfectly. And they're just as good now as they were then.

Makes about 2½ dozen cookies
Baking pan: greased cookie
   sheet
Preheat oven to 350°

¾ cup butter
½ cup sugar
1 egg
1½ teaspoons vanilla
2 cups flour
½ teaspoon salt
1 cup blanched almonds,
   ground fine
1 egg white
2 tablespoons sugar
green and red crystal sugar

1. Cream the butter and ½ cup of sugar.
2. Add the egg and vanilla and blend well.
3. Stir together the flour, salt and ground almonds. Add to the creamed mixture and blend well.
4. Turn the dough out onto a lightly floured board and knead for a few minutes or until the dough does not stick to your hands.
5. Break off a small piece of dough and roll it into a rope about the thickness of a pencil. The dough will be crumbly, so handle it carefully. Cut the rope down to 6 inches long and place it on the cookie sheet. Shape it into a ring with the ends overlapping as shown in the drawing. Repeat with the remaining dough, leaving 1½ inches between rings on the cookie sheet.
6. Beat the egg white until it is foamy. Add the 2 tablespoons of sugar and continue beating until the sugar is dissolved. Brush each ring with the egg white mixture and sprinkle with green or red crystal sugar.
7. Bake for 18 minutes. Allow the cookies to cool on the cookie sheet for a minute or two and then transfer them carefully to wire racks to finish cooling.

Gingerbread Angels

Follow the drawings step by step to make these mildly spicy Gingerbread Angels. All you need is a small bell cookie cutter, a small heart cutter and a round cutter about 1 inch in diameter. Glaze the cookies and then decorate with piped designs; before you start the decorations read about piping on pages 21–24.

Makes about 2½ dozen cookies
Baking pan: greased cookie sheet
Preheat oven to 350°

¾ cup margarine
½ cup brown sugar
½ cup molasses
½ cup dark corn syrup
2 eggs
5 cups flour
2 teaspoons baking soda
2 teaspoons ginger
1 teaspoon cinnamon
¼ teaspoon ground cloves
½ teaspoon nutmeg
1 egg white

Milk Glaze (page 165)
Decorating Icing (page 21)

1. Cream the margarine, brown sugar, molasses and corn syrup.
2. Add the eggs and blend well.
3. Stir together the flour, baking soda and spices. Add to the creamed mixture and blend well to make a smooth dough. Divide the dough in half, wrap each half snugly in plastic and refrigerate for 2 hours or until firm enough to roll out.
4. Dust the work surface and rolling pin with flour. Roll out half the dough at a time to a little less than ¼-inch thick. For each angel, cut out a small bell, a small heart and a plain round about 1 inch in diameter. Lift away the excess dough and save it for re-rolling.
5. Transfer one bell to the cookie sheet. Follow the steps in the drawing to make an angel right on the cookie sheet. Use dabs of egg white as glue and be sure to press the parts firmly together. Repeat this process to make more angels, leaving 2 inches between them on the cookie sheet.

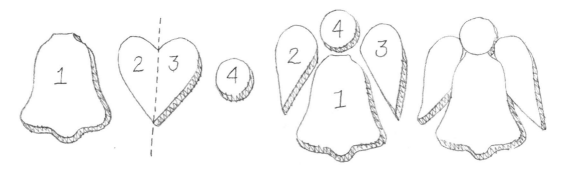

6. Bake for 15 minutes. Let the cookies cool on the cookie sheet for a minute or two and then transfer to wire racks to finish cooling.

7. Spread or paint a thin coat of Milk Glaze on each cookie and let it harden. Make simple piped decorations with Decorating Icing, following the drawings for ideas or inventing designs of your own. Be sure to read all about icing and piping on pages 21–24 before carrying out your decorating plans.

Pastel Spritz Cookies

Spritz cookies are made with a cookie press and a variety of templates (little disks that fit onto the end of the press); my cookie press came with a Christmas tree and a wreath as well as the standard heart, diamond, star and other disks. It's important to keep this dough refrigerated until you put it into the press; if the dough gets too warm and oozy while you are working, simply put the cookie press itself into the refrigerator for a little while and then continue.

Makes about 2½ dozen cookies
Baking pan: ungreased cookie
   sheet
Preheat oven to 325°

1 cup butter
¾ cup sugar
1 egg plus 1 egg yolk
1 teaspoon vanilla
2½ cups flour
red, green and yellow food
   coloring

For decorating:
candied cherries and other
   candied fruit, chocolate
   chips, nuts, small pieces of
   peppermint candy

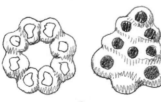

1. Cream the butter and sugar.
2. Add the egg, egg yolk and vanilla and blend well.
3. Add the flour gradually, blending well.
4. Divide the dough among three bowls. Color one bowl of dough with a few drops of red food coloring to make pink dough; color another bowl light green and color the third bowl yellow. Be sure to blend the food coloring into the dough very evenly. Cover the bowls with plastic wrap and refrigerate for 1 hour.
5. Take the pink dough out of the refrigerator and pack it into the cookie press with the template of your choice. Press cookies out on the cookie sheet, leaving 2 inches between them. If the dough begins to get too soft and runny, put the entire cookie press in the refrigerator until the dough has firmed up.

When the pink dough is used up, wash the press carefully so none of the pink will muddy the green or yellow dough.

If there is room on the cookie sheet, you may begin to make green cookies. If not, go right to step 6.
6. Decorate the pink cookies with fruit, chocolate chips, nuts or pieces of candy, checking the drawings for ideas or inventing designs of your own. Press the decorations firmly into the cookies.

7. Bake for 10 minutes. Watch the cookies carefully; they should not be browned. Let the cookies cool on the cookie sheet for a minute or two and then transfer to wire racks to finish cooling.

Repeat steps 5, 6 and 7 with the green dough and then with the yellow dough.

Florentines

Florentines are a variation of lace wafers, with walnuts, cherries and candied orange peel added and a chocolate coating on one side of the cookie. It's quite an extravaganza of flavors, easy to make once you get the hang of removing the sticky wafers from the cookie sheet.

Makes about 4½ dozen cookies
Baking pan: ungreased cookie
   sheet
Preheat oven to 350°

½ cup butter
6 tablespoons light corn syrup
½ cup brown sugar
¼ cup finely chopped walnuts
¼ cup chopped candied
   cherries
¼ cup chopped candied
   orange peel
1 tablespoon grated lemon rind
¾ cup plus 2 tablespoons flour
2 cups (12 ounces) chocolate
   chips, melted

1. Stir the butter, corn syrup and brown sugar in a saucepan over low heat until melted.

2. Add the walnuts, cherries, orange peel and grated lemon rind and blend well.

3. Add the flour and blend well.

4. Drop the dough by teaspoons onto the cookie sheet, leaving 3 inches between drops.

5. Bake for 8–10 minutes, until golden and flat. Let the cookies cool on the cookie sheet *for only a minute or two.* Use a spatula to loosen all the cookies at one time. Transfer the cookies to wire racks. If the cookies cool too much, you will not be able to detach them cleanly from the cookie sheet; in that case, return them to the oven to warm up and then continue removing them with the spatula.

6. When the cookies are cool, spread chocolate on the flat side of each cookie. Place the cookies, chocolate side up, on the wire racks and let the chocolate harden.

Chocolate Almond Pretzels

I confess to having favorites among my cookies, and this is one of them. If you happen to love rich, delicately almond-flavored dough, firm but soft, topped with chocolate and ground almonds—you'll just have to put this cookie on your top ten list.

Makes about 15 cookies
Baking pan: greased cookie
   sheet
Preheat oven to 375°

1 cup butter
1 cup sugar
2 eggs plus 1 egg yolk
¼ cup sour cream
1 teaspoon vanilla
¼ teaspoon almond extract
2½ cups flour
1 teaspoon baking powder
¼ teaspoon salt
¼ cup ground almonds (for the dough)
4 squares (4 ounces) semi-sweet chocolate
ground almonds (for the top of the cookies)

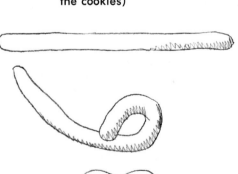

1. Cream the butter and sugar.

2. Add the eggs, egg yolk, sour cream, vanilla and almond extract and blend well.

3. Stir together the flour, baking powder, salt and ¼ cup of ground almonds. Add to the creamed mixture and blend well. Refrigerate the dough for 3 hours or until firm enough to handle.

4. Dust the work surface generously with flour. Break off a piece of dough and roll it into a rope 10 inches long and about ¼–⅜-inch in diameter. Lift the rope onto the cookie sheet and shape it into a pretzel as shown in the drawing. Repeat with the remaining dough, leaving 2 inches between pretzels. If the dough gets too sticky to handle, return it to the refrigerator to firm up.

5. Bake for 12–13 minutes. The pretzels should remain pale; do not let them brown. Allow them to cool slightly on the cookie sheet and then transfer to wire racks.

6. While the cookies are baking, prepare the semi-sweet chocolate for brushing on the cookies, as described on the next page. When the cookies have been transferred to the wire racks and while they are still warm, paint the top of each one with a thin coat of melted chocolate (a small pastry brush is handy for this) and sprinkle immediately with ground almonds. Let the chocolate harden.

Preparing the chocolate

Melt the squares of chocolate in a heavy saucepan over very low heat, stirring. When the chocolate is almost melted, turn off the heat and stir until it is completely melted. Add ½ table-spoon of warm water and stir well. The chocolate will get quite thick and somewhat tight. Add an-other ½ tablespoon of water and stir briskly; the chocolate will begin to thin out. Add 2 more tablespoons of water, ½ tablespoon at a time, stirring after each addition, to thin the chocolate sufficiently for brushing.

Gingerbread Wreaths

These big, beautiful wreaths are made of very spicy gin-gerbread, coated with punchy Rum Glaze before you add the lavish decorations—raisins, candied fruit, dates, even whole almonds and pecans. They should taste as rich as a fruit cake and look twice as festive. Each cookie is a complete dessert. Merry Christmas!

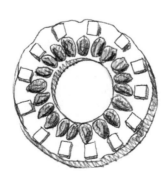

Makes about 3 dozen cookies
Baking pan: ungreased cookie
    sheet
Preheat oven to 350°

½ cup margarine
½ cup sugar
½ cup molasses
1 egg
2½–3 cups flour
1½ teaspoons baking soda
½ teaspoon salt
1½ teaspoons cinnamon
1 teaspoon ginger
½ teaspoon ground cloves

Rum Glaze (page 166)

For decorating:
whole almonds, pecans and
    pine nuts
raisins, dates and dried fruit
candied cherries and other
    candied fruit

1. Cream the margarine, sugar and molasses.

2. Add the egg and blend well.

3. Stir together 2½ cups of the flour, the baking soda, salt and spices. Add to the creamed mixture and blend well. If the dough seems sticky, gradually add the remaining ½ cup flour until the dough is smooth. Divide the dough in half, wrap each half snugly in plastic and refrigerate for 2 hours or until the dough is firm enough to roll out.

4. To make the wreaths you will need one large round cookie cutter 3½ inches in diameter and one smaller round cookie cutter 1½ inches in diameter.

Dust the work surface and rolling pin with flour. Roll out half the dough at a time to a little less than ¼-inch thick. Cut the rolled dough with the larger cutter and then cut a small round from the center of each large round. Lift away the excess dough and save it for re-rolling. Transfer the wreaths to the cookie sheet, leaving 1 inch between them.

5. Bake for 8–10 minutes. Let the cookies cool on the cookie sheet for a minute or two and then transfer to wire racks to finish cooling.

6. Decorate the cookies one at a time: Spread a wreath with Rum Glaze. Decorate, using the drawings for guidance or inventing your own designs. Be sure to press each nut, raisin or piece of fruit firmly into the soft glaze. Let the glaze harden.

Sugar Cookie Ornaments

If you plan to use these cookies as ornaments on your Christmas tree, make plenty of them because I can assure you some of them will disappear into the mouths of hungry tree-trimmers. Each cookie is topped with another smaller cookie, so you'll need some small cutters—aspic or canapé cutters, miniature hearts, tiny gingerbread people.

Makes about 3½ dozen cookies
Baking pan: greased cookie
   sheet
Preheat oven to 350°

1½ cups margarine or butter
1 cup sugar
2 eggs
3 tablespoons milk
1 teaspoon vanilla
3¼ cups flour
1 teaspoon baking powder
½ teaspoon salt

For decorating:
1 egg white mixed with 1
   teaspoon water
colored sugar or colored dots

1. Cream the margarine and sugar.

2. Add the eggs, milk and vanilla and blend well.

3. Stir together the flour, baking powder, and salt. Add to the creamed mixture and blend well. Divide the dough in three parts, wrap each part snugly in plastic and refrigerate for 2 hours or until firm enough to roll out.

4. Before you roll out the dough, collect a round cookie cutter approximately 2½ inches in diameter and a few smaller cutters in decorative shapes; check the drawings for guidance.

Dust the work surface and rolling pin with flour. Roll out one piece of dough at a time to ⅛-inch thick. For each cookie ornament, cut one large round and one smaller decorative shape. Lift away the excess dough and save it for re-rolling. Transfer the rounds to the cookie sheet.

5. Use a plastic straw to make a hole near the top of each round.

6. Brush each round with egg white. Center the decorative shapes on the rounds and sprinkle the rounds with colored sugar or colored dots. Blow away the excess sugar or dots.

7. Bake for 13 minutes or until golden. While the cookies are still hot, reopen the holes with the straw. Transfer the cookies to wire racks to cool.

To hang the cookie ornaments, simply slip short lengths of yarn or string through the holes and tie to the tree.

Cinnamon Sweethearts

Each big cookie is actually made up of four smaller hearts, a nice way to give your valentine a little something extra. Decorate with cinnamon redhots pressed firmly into the cookie dough. Pack a gift of these cookies in a white box lined with red tissue paper, tied with red and pink ribbons.

Makes about 1 dozen cookies, depending on the size of the cookie cutter used
Baking pan: greased cookie sheet
Preheat oven to 350°

1 cup butter or margarine
¾ cup sugar
2 hard-cooked egg yolks
1 egg plus 1 egg yolk
1 teaspoon grated lemon rind
3 cups flour
½ teaspoon salt
½ teaspoon cinnamon
1 egg white mixed with 1 teaspoon water
sugar and cinnamon mixed together to taste
cinnamon redhots

1. Cream the butter and sugar.
2. Mash the hard-cooked yolks and add them, along with the raw eggs and the grated lemon rind, to the creamed mixture. Blend well.
3. Stir together the flour, salt and cinnamon. Add to the creamed mixture and blend well. Divide the dough in half, wrap each half snugly in plastic and refrigerate for 2 hours or until firm enough to roll out.
4. Dust the work surface and rolling pin with flour. Roll out half the dough at a time to ⅛-inch thick. Brush the dough with egg white and sprinkle lightly and evenly with the sugar and cinnamon mixture. Use a small cookie cutter to cut hearts as shown in the drawing. If you cut the dough carefully, there will be very little excess.
5. Transfer four hearts to the cookie sheet and arrange them as shown to make one Cinnamon Sweetheart. Press and push the edges together gently but firmly. Decorate with cinnamon redhots. Repeat with the remaining hearts, leaving 2–3 inches between the completed cookies.
6. Bake for 10–12 minutes. Let the cookies cool slightly on the cookie sheet and then transfer carefully to wire racks to finish cooling.

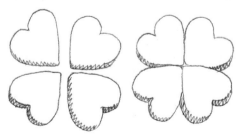

Chocolate Shortbread Hearts

How could your true love resist you if you sent a St. Valentine's Day gift of beautiful Chocolate Shortbread Hearts? Each rich cookie is coated with semi-sweet chocolate and decorated with candied violets and bits of green candied cherries.

Makes about 3½ dozen cookies
Baking pan: ungreased cookie sheet
Preheat oven to 325°

1 cup butter, almost room temperature
¾ cup confectioners' sugar
2¼ cups flour
3 tablespoons unsweetened cocoa (not cocoa mix)
½ teaspoon salt
6 squares (6 ounces) semi-sweet chocolate, melted
candied violets
green candied cherries

1. Cream the butter until light. Add the confectioners' sugar gradually and continue beating until the mixture is fluffy.

2. Stir together the flour, cocoa and salt. Add to the creamed mixture and work it in with your hands, blending well. Divide the dough in half, wrap each half snugly in plastic and refrigerate until the dough is firm enough to roll.

3. Dust the work surface and rolling pin with flour and roll out half the dough at a time to about ⅛-inch thick. Cut with a heart cookie cutter about 2–2½ inches high. Gather up the excess dough and save it for re-rolling. Use a spatula to transfer the hearts carefully to the cookie sheet, leaving 1 inch between them.

4. Bake for 15 minutes. Let the hearts cool very slightly on the cookie sheet and then transfer to wire racks.

5. While the cookies are still warm, spread the tops with melted chocolate. Decorate with candied violets and small pieces of green candied cherries as shown in the drawing, pressing the decorations into the soft chocolate.

Linzer Hearts

Send a message of love with these thin, crisp, delicate cookies sandwiched together with raspberry preserves. They are as pretty as valentines, the tops sprinkled with confectioners' sugar and red jam peeking through the heart-shaped windows.

Makes about 2 dozen
   sandwiches (4 dozen
   cookies)
Baking pan: ungreased cookie
   sheet
Preheat oven to 350°

¾ cup butter
1 cup sugar
2 eggs
1 teaspoon vanilla
2½ cups flour
1 teaspoon baking powder
½ teaspoon salt
raspberry jam
confectioners' sugar

1. Cream the butter and sugar.
2. Add the eggs and vanilla and blend well.
3. Stir together the flour, baking powder and salt. Add to the creamed mixture and blend well. Divide the dough in thirds, wrap each part snugly in plastic and refrigerate for several hours or until firm enough to roll out.
4. Turn a cookie sheet over and sprinkle the back with flour. Roll out one third of the dough at a time to ⅛-inch thick, right on the back of the cookie sheet. Chill the rolled dough for 10 minutes. Using a cookie cutter about 3 inches wide and 2½ inches high, cut an even number of hearts, leaving 1 inch between them. Carefully lift away the excess dough and save it for re-rolling. Using a tiny heart-shaped cutter, cut hearts in the centers of half the cookies, as shown in the drawing. Lift the small hearts away and add them to the excess dough.
5. Bake for 12 minutes. Watch the cookies very carefully to be sure they don't burn. Let them cool slightly on the cookie sheet and then transfer to wire racks to finish cooling.
6. Spread jam on the whole hearts. Cover each with a cut-out heart. Sprinkle with confectioners' sugar sifted through a fine strainer.

Fancy Easter Eggs

There's nothing prettier than a fancy Easter egg, unless it's a fancy Easter egg cookie. Decorate these cookies either with piped designs or more simply with colored sprinkles, dots and candies. The drawings show you lots of designs and you will surely come up with some of your own designs, too.

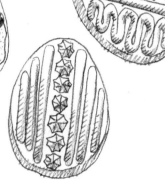

Makes about 4 dozen cookies
Baking pan: ungreased cookie
   sheet
Preheat oven to 375°

1 cup butter or margarine
1 cup sugar
1 teaspoon vanilla
2 tablespoons milk
2½ cups flour
¼ teaspoon salt

For decorating:
Milk Glaze (page 165) or
   Lemon Glaze (page 166)
Decorating Icing (page 21)
assorted sprinkles, dots and
   candies of your choice

1. Cream the butter and sugar.

2. Add the vanilla and milk and blend well.

3. Stir together the flour and salt. Add gradually to the creamed mixture, blending well. As the dough gets stiffer, you may find it easier to work the flour in with your hands. Divide the dough into thirds, wrap each part snugly in plastic and refrigerate for 2 hours or until firm enough to roll out.

4. Dust the work surface and rolling pin with flour. Roll out one third of the dough at a time to a little less than ¼-inch thick. Cut with an oval cookie cutter or a round cutter that you have bent into an oval. Lift away the excess dough and save it for re-rolling. Transfer the cookies to the cookie sheet, leaving 1½ inches between them.

5. Bake for 10–12 minutes, until the edges are golden. Watch the cookies carefully to be sure they don't brown. Let the cookies cool slightly on

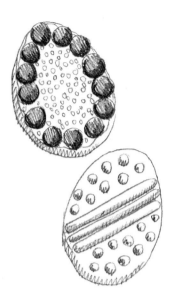

the cookie sheet and then transfer them to wire racks to finish cooling.

6. There are two ways to decorate the Easter egg cookies: with piped designs made of Decorating Icing or with sprinkles, dots and candies.

To decorate with piped designs, first spread or paint Milk Glaze or Lemon Glaze on the cookies. Let it harden to make the foundation for the piping. Read pages 21–24 to find out all about coloring the icing and how to make piped designs. Pipe the designs, following the drawings for guidance or inventing your own designs.

To decorate with sprinkles, dots and candies, spread only two cookies at a time with Milk Glaze or Lemon Glaze and quickly apply sprinkles or dots before the glaze dries. Press candies into the moist glaze. Continue in this fashion until all the cookies are decorated.

GLAZES

Milk Glaze

Makes about ⅔ cup

2 cups confectioners' sugar
3 tablespoons hot milk
2 teaspoons vanilla

Combine the ingredients and blend until smooth.

Vanilla Glaze

Makes about ½ cup

1 tablespoon butter
½ teaspoon vanilla
2½ tablespoons milk
1½ cups sifted confectioners' sugar
pinch of salt

Melt the butter. Turn off the heat, add the vanilla and milk and stir. Add the confectioners' sugar and salt and blend until smooth. The glaze should be liquid but quite thick. If you want to thin it, add a little more milk.

Chocolate Glaze

Makes about ½ cup

1 tablespoon butter
1 square (1 ounce) unsweetened chocolate
1 cup confectioners' sugar
1 tablespoon milk
1 tablespoon water
½ teaspoon vanilla

Melt the butter and chocolate in a heavy saucepan over very low heat. Add about ⅓ cup of the confectioners' sugar and stir. In a cup, stir together the milk, water and vanilla. Add that and the remaining confectioners' sugar to the chocolate mixture and stir. Blend all the ingredients with a wire whisk until very smooth.

You may thin the glaze with small amounts of water to maintain the consistency needed for the recipe.

Rum Glaze

Makes about 1¼ cups

2½ cups confectioners' sugar
½ cup light rum
2 teaspoons vanilla

Mix the ingredients together until smooth. If the glaze seems too thick for easy spreading, add another teaspoon or two of rum or water.

Lemon Glaze

Makes about ¾ cup

¼ cup lemon juice
1 teaspoon vanilla
1¼ cups confectioners' sugar

Stir the ingredients together and blend until smooth.

Mocha Glaze

Makes about 1 cup

2 squares (2 ounces)
    unsweetened chocolate
2 tablespoons butter
1⅓ cups confectioners' sugar
pinch of salt
4 tablespoons hot coffee
½ teaspoon vanilla

Melt the chocolate and butter in a heavy saucepan over low heat, stirring constantly. In a bowl, stir together the confectioners' sugar, salt, coffee and vanilla. Add the chocolate mixture to the sugar mixture and beat until smooth. If necessary, you may thin the glaze with a little more coffee.

INDEX

Have BETTER HOMES & GARDENS® magazine
delivered to your door. For information, write to:
Mr. ROBERT AUSTIN, P.O. Box 4536,
DES MOINES, IOWA 50336